TEACHERS
AND THE
TEACHING
AUTHORITIES

TEACHERS AND THE TEACHING AUTHORITIES

W. A.Visser 't Hooft

WCC Publications, Geneva

Cover design: Rob Lucas

ISBN 2-8254-1330-5

© 2000 WCC Publications, World Council of Churches
150 route de Ferney, P.O. Box 2100
1211 Geneva 2, Switzerland
Website: http://www.wcc-coe.org

Printed in Switzerland

Contents

vii   Foreword   *Alan Falconer*

1   1.   Introduction

3   2.   Teachers in the New Testament

6   3.   Teachers Decrease – Bishops Increase

9   4.   Teachers at Carthage and Alexandria

11   5.   Episcopal Teachers

14   6.   A *Magisterium* of the *Magistri* ?

19   7.   *Magistri* as Reformers

25   8.   The *Magisterium* in the Context of Papal Infallibility

30   9.   The Threat of Divorce between the *Magistri* and the *Magisterium*

35   10.   Theologians Rediscover the Church

41   11.   The *Magistri* Participate in the *Magisterium*

44   12.   Once More the Parting of the Ways ?

52   13.   Authority and Freedom in Eastern Orthodoxy

56   14.   *Magistri* and *Magisterium* in the Ecumenical Dialogue

64   15.   *Magistri* as the Fourth Office ?

68   16.   Conclusion

Foreword

Willem Adolf Visser 't Hooft was the first general secretary of the World Council of Churches, and one of the leading figures in the 20th-century ecumenical movement. Born on 20 September 1900 in Haarlem, Netherlands, he was to become associated with every significant ecumenical initiative in the century – the Student Christian Movement, the Young Men's Christian Association, the Life and Work movement, Faith and Order, and the World Student Christian Federation. In each of these he played a central role, and thus became the inevitable choice for the post of general secretary of the World Council of Churches in process of formation and, then, of the World Council of Churches itself.

Although he was a Reformed pastor who wrote some fifteen books in several languages, he did not consider himself to be a theologian, but rather one whose writings on theological subjects should be regarded as "interpretations across confessional and linguistic frontiers of thoughts... picked up from the theological pathfinders".

But who were these theological pathfinders and how did they relate to the authorities of the different churches? Many theologians active in ecumenical reflection and central to the development of the ecumenical movement itself found themselves on the boundary of their church. What was therefore the role of the theologian in seeking to discern and articulate the word of God for and to the church in each time and each place?

Throughout his life, Willem Visser 't Hooft wrestled with these questions. They are, after all, fundamental for ecumenical *processes*. Who has the authority to speak for the different churches in ecumenical dialogue? Is the representative role of the participants in different dialogues primarily to state the positions of the different churches, or are the participants enabled and empowered to discern and explore avenues of agreement and convergence, even in advance of the churches? These questions so exercised Visser 't Hooft that he was still exploring them in writing only days before his death.

It is therefore fitting, as an aspect of the celebration of his birth one hundred years ago, that this, his final manuscript, be published in full (an abridged version already appeared in *The Ecumenical Review,* vol. 38, no. 2, 1986, pp.152ff.). This text is a good example of the breadth and depth of Visser 't Hooft's theological engagement. His canvas is large. The major trends on each issue, evident throughout the history of the church, are presented and analyzed. The insights and wrestlings of each confessional tradition are explored. Individual theologians who have gone beyond their authorities but who have remained central to the life and witness of the church, e.g. Tertullian, are identified to demonstrate that that which is not acceptable in one time and place may be of central importance for a later generation.

Throughout this work two strong convictions of Visser 't Hooft are evident in particular. As with many of his other works (e.g. *Rembrandt and the Bible),* the testimony of scripture is normative. Although he does not go as far as Gerhard Ebeling did in his declaration that "church history is the history of the exposition of scripture", Visser 't Hooft decisively affirms – in consonance with Karl Barth – that the task of the teachers *(magistri)* is threefold – the interpretation of scripture; unfolding the faith in a systematic manner; and the application of that faith to the problems of daily life.

A second conviction punctuating the pages of this work is that theology is dialogical. The task of the teacher and of the ecumenical theologian is not simply to restate the positions adopted by the churches or Christian confessional traditions, but to engage in a journey of discovery together. For Visser 't Hooft, the ultimate aim of the ecumenical movement is unity. He is reputed to have observed: "The aim is not dialogue, but unity. Our Lord did not pray that they may all enter into conversations with one another: he prayed that they may be one." This dialogue which could lead to unity was not, however, an attempt to build something new, but was a return to the sources, or still better, a return to the centre, Jesus Christ. The task of each church is to encourage dialogue – including dialogue between the *magistri* and the *magisterium* – precisely so that the focus of the church is *that* centre, and not issues which, though important, are peripheral to it.

Although this book emerges from an unfinished manuscript which is now nearly twenty years old, its publication is not merely a fitting testimony to the insights and theological acumen of one of the great pioneers of the ecumenical movement. While that in itself would have undoubtedly warranted the publication of this manuscript as a centennial tribute, the book makes an important contribution to an ongoing ecumenical debate within and between the churches. The reaction of theologians to the signing of the joint declaration between the Lutheran World Federation and the Roman Catholic Church in 1999 once again posed existentially the question of the relation between the *magistri* and the *magisterium*. The major theological work on *The Nature and Purpose of the Church* which is being conducted by the WCC's commission on Faith and Order has also begun to address the question of authoritative teaching and the teaching authority of the church, and will do so again in a major consultation being planned for 2002. This volume will help to inform that study, as Visser 't Hooft, with his uncanny vision, raised fundamental questions and suggested perspectives which may help the churches through the commission to move towards convergence.

The publication of *Teachers and the Teaching Authorities* is therefore a fitting tribute to the memory of Willem Adolf Visser 't Hooft, demonstrating as it does his perspicacity in identifying and addressing issues which continue to exercise the churches as they seek that unity for which our Lord prayed.

> ALAN D. FALCONER
> Director
> Commission on Faith and Order

Editorial note: The manuscript is published as it was written, in the mid-1980s, and no attempt has been made to update the language.

1. Introduction

From the first centuries A.D., and through all the history of the Christian church, one fundamental question has continually arisen – what is the proper relationship between the *magistri*, or theological teachers, and the *magisterium*, the authority which decides what is the true teaching of the church? In other words, are the *magistri* simply mouth-pieces of the *magisterium* and completely subject to its control, or do they form part of the *magisterium*, sharing its responsibility for establishing true teaching? Or again, is there a third possible position, between the two just mentioned?

In spite of the great importance of this question in the history of the church, it has never received an answer that all considered fully adequate and definitive. Again and again, situations of tension and conflict have developed in which the *magistri* and the *magisterium* have found themselves in opposition. The problem has become particularly acute in our time and there is, to my knowledge, no church today in which it has not arisen in some form or another. I think it is no exaggeration to say that the tension between theologians and church authorities, be these the papacy, bishops or synods, is greater today than it has ever been.

This issue is, of course, of vital importance to the ecumenical movement, and forms one of the most difficult items on its agenda. Churches which have a similar conception of the Christian faith are not infrequently separated by their understanding of the nature and role of the *magisterium*. The question raises a practical difficulty in the ecumenical life of the churches, when it has to be decided what place should be given in the ecumenical dialogue to those theologians who go further than the authorities of their own churches in their search for a solution to the problem of church unity, or who take a critical attitude to the position of these authorities.

Perhaps the question should be put in a wider context. In the ecclesiastical history of our time, the churches have ceased to be monolithic. Father Yves Congar's statement that the Roman Catholic Church "no longer presents a monolithic unity" is true of all churches.[1] In a certain sense they have all become pluralistic, and it has to be asked how the right balance can be ensured between the official dialogue of the churches and unofficial dialogue between theological groups and individual theologians.

NOTE

[1] In *Voices of Unity*, Geneva, WCC, 1981, p.24.

2. Teachers in the New Testament

The problem of the relationship between theologians and church authorities arose for the first time on St Paul's two visits to the leaders of the church in Jerusalem, as described in the first chapters of the epistle to the Galatians. Paul was a fully trained theologian whose great gift, or *charisma*, was his ability to preach and expound the content of the new faith at a high intellectual level and with profound insight. In Jerusalem, he was confronted with Galilean fishermen who had had little education, but who had the spiritual authority of men who had been in daily contact with the Lord Jesus Christ. The difficulty and delicacy of the situation are indicated by his admission that he feared he might be "running in vain",[1] that is, that he would remain an outsider rather than become a full member of the family of God. Paul was very conscious of the importance of the leaders in Jerusalem, and sincerely desired to be in complete communion with them. At the same time, he made it very clear that he was not ready to consider them as the ultimate judges and arbiters of the message and mission of the church. They were "reported to be pillars",[2] and Paul did not deny this. But he also said, "They were reported to be something – what they were makes no difference to me."[3] That is to say, they were not important because they had certain positions or titles; they were important in that they were true witnesses of the Lord.

Paul came to Jerusalem with the conviction that, since the believer is justified by faith, he is liberated from the prescriptions of the Law. As a theologian, he had fully considered the implications of the freedom which the gospel offers. The leaders in Jerusalem had probably not drawn this far-reaching conclusion, in order not to endanger their already very difficult relations with the Jewish authorities. In spite of this, they did not ask Paul to change his policy, but simply requested him to participate in the collection for the poor in Jerusalem. Paul was glad to do this, and all concerned confirmed their fellowship with one another. The understanding so reached was not invalidated by the fact that Peter later broke this agreement by his "inconsistent" or "insincere" behaviour in Antioch. Paul continued to attach great importance to the collection for Jerusalem as a sign that he conceived his mission as part of the total mission of the church which had had its origin in Jerusalem. Thus the theologian and the church authorities showed that their relationship could take the form of a recognition of the specific calling of each of the partners, and need not be endangered by conflict about precedence and power.

We must now consider the place of teachers in the young church, where they appear on the scene at a very early stage. At Antioch, which became the most active centre of missionary activity, the congregation was led by prophets and teachers.[4] These teachers, together with the apostles, formed the backbone of church life and church order in Paul's time. They were "charismatics"; that is, they were not elected officials, but men who had received a specific gift of grace which the Christian community recognized. They were maintained by the community in accordance with the principle, "Let him who is taught the word share all good things with him who teaches."[5] To be a teacher was therefore a full-time calling. In the first epistle to the Corinthians, Paul enumerated various charismatic callings: "God has appointed in the church first apostles, second prophets, third teachers."[6] In the epistle to the Romans, the gifts of prophecy, service and teaching head the list.[7] In the epistle to the Ephesians, the order is apostles, prophets, evangelists, pastors and teachers.[8] Teachers were highly respected, as they shared the authority of the original Teacher, the Rabbi and *Didaskalos* who "spoke with authority and not as the scribes".[9] Therefore no one could become a teacher unless he had been called by God to this task. In the epistle of James we find the warning, "Let not many of you become teachers, my brethren, for you know that we who teach shall be judged with greater strictness."[10]

As to the functions of a teacher, we do not find in the New Testament an explicit definition of the task, but we have enough illustrations to shed some light on the question. The gospel of St Matthew, pre-eminently concerned with the teaching task of the church, is an excellent example of that teaching as addressed to a wider audience. The three principal areas of teaching are described as, first, the interpretation of the scriptures in such a way that the coming of Jesus is seen to be their fulfilment; second, the unfolding of the faith in a systematic manner; and third, the application of that faith to the problems of daily life.

Paul himself was the foremost teacher[11] and other teachers tried to follow his example. Later, only a few, as for example the author of the epistle to the Hebrews, who according to Luther may have been the learned Alexandrian Apollos, were able to share with their hearers as deep and original an insight into the meaning of the faith as Paul had given, many offering "milk" rather than "solid food".

During the years of Paul's missionary activity, teachers were considered to be responsible for the transmission of the *didachē*, that is, the content and meaning of the faith. What we learn of other leaders in the church at that time, such as deacons, presbyters and overseers *(episkopoi)*, seems to indicate that they had other tasks to fulfill. It is surprising therefore that in the pastoral epistles, which most scholars consider to be the writings of St Paul's pupils rather than his own, teaching is said to be the responsibility of overseers and presbyters. The overseer or *episkopos*, who seems to have had an administrative function in St Paul's time, is here described as a man who must be able to teach[12] or as one able to give instruction in sound doctrine *(didaskalia)*.[13] This clearly reduces the importance of the full-time teacher as the one leader entrusted with the teaching office.

NOTES

[1] Gal. 2:2.
[2] Gal. 2:9.
[3] Gal. 2:6.
[4] Acts 13:1.
[5] Gal. 6:6, see also *Didache* 13:2.
[6] 1 Cor. 12:28.
[7] Rom. 12:6-7.
[8] Eph. 4:11.
[9] Mark 1:22.
[10] James 3:1.
[11] Acts 13:1; 1 Tim. 2:7; 2 Tim. 1:11.
[12] 1 Tim. 3:2.
[13] Titus 1:9.

3. Teachers Decrease – Bishops Increase

The importance of the full-time teacher was to be further reduced in the next period, which is roughly the last decade of the first century and the first half of the 2nd. The first letter of Clement of Rome, written to the Christians in Corinth, deals with the problem of the relations between church leaders and other members of the church. Even though Paul, in his dealings with the Corinthians, had so strongly emphasized the role of the teachers, Clement speaks only of presbyters and over-seers, *episkopoi* who were in fact bishops, though not yet monarchical bishops. A partial explanation for this is to be found in the *Didache*, the teaching of the twelve apostles, a church manual of the late first or early 2nd century. In the local churches for which this manual was written, the teachers still played an important role, and appear to have moved from one congregation to another to carry it out. The churches were urged to welcome "as the Lord" teachers who came to them "furthering the Lord's righteousness and knowledge".[1] They were, however, also urged to elect bishops and deacons, "for their ministry is identical with that of the prophets and teachers", and they "enjoy along with the prophets and teachers a place of honour among you".[2] We have here an explicit state-ment that the task which the teachers had hitherto fulfilled was to devolve also on the holders of other offices. An important reason for this development may have been the fact that the eucharist was by this time celebrated every Sunday, and could not be prepared and administered by teachers alone, but required the appointment of local office-bearers. Edward Schillebeeckx remarks on this subject: "The bishops *(episkopoi)* and their helpers are here in the service of the prophets and teachers, who continue to preside in the liturgy. These newcomers share in the liturgi-cal leadership or in the ministry of the prophets and teachers."[3]

In other 2nd-century writings we find that the teacher had practically disappeared as an office-bearer, and that the bishop (at first several bish-ops in each place, then one local bishop) had taken his place. In a letter concerning the martyrdom of Polycarp, bishop of Smyrna, he is called "an apostolic and prophetic teacher and bishop",[4] and later "a noble teacher".[5] The theological basis for this concentration on the office of the bishop is given by Ignatius of Antioch. He declared that the faithful should regard the bishop as the Lord himself,[6] and went on to say: "Let the bishop preside in God's place."[7] He exhorted the Smyrnaeans to do nothing without the bishop's approval,[8] and warned the Philadelphians to flee from schism and false teaching *(kakodidaskalia)* by remaining obedient to the bishop and following their shepherd like sheep.[9]

Later in the 2nd century, Irenaeus developed this conception of the church: "The bishops, the *ecclesia docens*, are explicitly guardians of the Christian doctrine."[10] According to Irenaeus, the apostles handed down to their successors, that is, to the bishops, "their own teaching position",[11] giving the bishops authority to teach. Although the expression was not used, they were to be the bearers of the *magisterium*.

It is a far cry from St Paul to the church leaders of the 2nd century. At the start, the teachers had been considered the leaders. In the new situation, the leaders were considered to be the chief teachers. The *episkopos*, who had had only a minor role in the early days, had come to occupy centre stage; and the teacher, who had at first been one of the chief charismatic leaders, was no longer mentioned among the men who bore responsibility for the spiritual welfare of the church.

We have not enough evidence to enable us to explain adequately why this great change had taken place, but we can mention the most probable reasons. One was obviously that the local congregation needed a leader who could preside regularly at its services, particularly at the celebration of holy communion. The charismatic teachers were for the most part itinerant, and therefore could not fulfill this particular function, though it may well be that in some cases the teacher had become "localized" and was transformed into an *episkopos*.[12] Secondly, as Hans Lietzmann suggests in his *Geschichte der alten Kirche*, the church needed strong unified leadership in its struggle against gnosticism and paganism.[13] A third reason was the increasing institutionalization of the church. The original church order, based on a symphony of varied charismatic gifts, had been replaced by a centralized and streamlined form of organization, dominated by the bishops. According to Adolf von Harnack, this was the decisive factor in the eclipse of the teaching ministry. The bishops could not tolerate a form of ministry which was not subordinated to the episcopate.[14]

NOTES

[1] *Didache* 11:1-2.
[2] *Didache* 15:1-2.
[3] Edward Schillebeeckx, *Kerkelijk ambt*, p. 32.
[4] Martyrdom of Polycarp 16:2.
[5] 19:1.
[6] Ephesians 6:1.
[7] Magnesians 6:1.
[8] Smyrnaeans 8:1.
[9] Philadelphians 2:1.
[10] Ellen Flesseman-van Leer, *Tradition and Scripture in the Early Church*, Assen, Van Gorcum, 1954, p.112.
[11] *Adversus Haereses* III:3:1.
[12] Adolf von Harnack, *The Constitution and Law of the Church*, New York, Putnam, 1910, p.93.
[13] Hans Lietzmann, *Geschichte der alten Kirche*, Berlin, W. de Gruyter, 1952-53, II:48.
[14] Adolf von Harnack, *Mission und Ausbreitung*, Leipzig, Hinrichs, 1902, p.345.

4. Teachers at Carthage and Alexandria

The 3rd century saw a continuation of the process whereby the old church order, based on a multiformity of spiritual gifts, was replaced by one of greater uniformity, the foundation of which was the episcopate, and very little more is heard of the role of teachers. There are, however, some very remarkable exceptions to this rule. It is as if, just when the era of the largely independent teachers came to an end, a demonstration was given of the very great contribution which such teachers could make to the life of the church.

One teacher who followed his own specific vocation, even when this meant disagreement with the official leadership of the church, was Tertullian, a lawyer in Carthage who became a presbyter and who wrote many books. His great concern was the purity of the church, so that he was attracted to the Montanist sect, with its strict moral discipline. Because of his extraordinary intellectual and spiritual gifts, he has continued to this day to exert a very strong influence on the church, and is widely recognized as one of its greatest teachers. Jerome reported that Cyprian read a portion of Tertullian's writings every day, saying to his servant, when the moment had come, "Bring me my master" *[Da magistrum]*.

In this period the best-known examples of men whose lives were wholly devoted to teaching are Clement Alexandrinus and Origen of the "School of Catechesis" in Alexandria. It is not easy to define the nature of this school. It seems to have been a successful combination of what we might call a confirmation class, a Bible school, a Sunday school for people of all ages, a graduate school of theology and a centre for courses on apologetics – all held together by the genius of Clement and Origen. As von Harnack stresses again and again when speaking of Origen, it was at this time that theology became a science. The whole intellectual heritage of Greece was applied to the clarification of the Christian faith. The foundation was, however, the Bible, so that biblical exegesis was the centre of this educational process. Christianity was no longer presented as the enemy of philosophy, as it had been regarded by Tertullian. It was recognized as the true *gnosis*, in which the aspirations of Greek culture were fulfilled. Christian teaching was not "good news" only for simple people, but also for thinkers. It is not surprising that this bold teaching presented by a brilliant young man fascinated the intelligentsia of Alexandria. It was, however, precisely this success which created trouble. The bishop of Alexandria condemned Origen, arguing that he had transgressed the rules of the church. There is some evidence too that there was a difference of opinion between Origen and the bishop on certain theological points. Both Jerome and Eusebius, however, believed that the bishop "could not endure the magnificence of [Origen's] eloquence and knowledge".[1]

The story of Origen highlights the ambivalence of the position of teachers. Here we have one of the greatest theologians of all time, who was invited by many bishops to advise on theological disputes arising in their dioceses. How he performed this difficult task can be seen from the account of his "Dialogue with Heraclides", a bishop whose orthodoxy had been called into question. Henry Chadwick comments: "The bishops did not, perhaps, trust their own powers to deal with such advanced theological questions."[2] Origen had to endeavour not to come again into conflict with the hierarchy. He therefore wrote: "With the permission of God and secondly of the bishops, thirdly of the presbyters and also of the people, I will again say what I think on this subject."[3] The key words in this statement are those concerning the permission of the bishops. Origen was expected to be grateful that he was allowed to address a meeting at which bishops were present. On an earlier occasion, Bishop Demetrius had insisted that teachers were not to speak in the presence of bishops.[4] The bishops of Jerusalem and Caesarea had disagreed with him, and had cited a number of cases in which teachers had spoken when bishops were present. They represented the past, however, and the strictly hierarchical point of view became the general rule.[5] Origen was therefore at the same time the last of the independent teachers and the founder of theology as a science.

NOTES

[1] Henry Chadwick, *Alexandrian Christianity*, Christian Classics, Philadelphia, Westminster, 1954, p.432.
[2] *Ibid.*
[3] *Ibid.*, p.440.
[4] Stephen Neill, *The Layman in Christian History*, London, SCM Press, 1963, p.42.
[5] Von Harnack, *Mission und Ausbreitung*, p.344.

5. Episcopal Teachers

Lietzmann says that the Eastern church loved and revered Origen passionately for two centuries, and then condemned him as a heretic in the next.[1] The men who followed Origen were, however, not independent teachers or schoolmen, and here we enter a long period of church history in which theology was in the hands of the bishops. As Yves Congar says, from about the 4th century onwards, the theologians were usually bishops and the outstanding bishops were theologians. The three great theologians known as the "ecumenical teachers", Gregory of Nazianzus, Gregory of Nyssa and Basil the Great, were all bishops, as were John Chrysostom and Athanasius.

It is interesting and impressive to note that several of these hierarchs made it very clear that they owed a great debt to Origen, even though he had been "only" a teacher, and though some of his theological opinions had been severely criticized. Basil the Great and Gregory of Nazianzus produced an anthology of Origen's writings, and John Chrysostom was condemned by a local council for defending Origen's orthodoxy. By 543, when Origen was finally declared to be a heretic, his thought had penetrated through many channels into the life of the church.

By this time, the teaching authority had become episcopal in the strictest sense of the word. The great ecumenical councils were synods of bishops, and we do not hear that theologians not belonging to the hierarchy participated fully in these deliberations, as they did later at the council of Constance. There is also no evidence that *periti*, or expert theologians, drafted the decrees issued, as was to be the case later at the Second Vatican Council. In fact, the theologian who has been called the "last of the church fathers", John of Damascus, was not a bishop but a monk.

In the West after the time of Tertullian the outstanding teachers, Cyprian, Ambrose and Augustine, shared Origen's deep attachment to the Bible, his concern that the Christian faith should be rightly interpreted to the surrounding cultural world, and his conception of theology as a creative science. Far more than Origen did, however, Augustine followed the lead of St Paul, and the quality as well as the quantity of his writings are such that they will long continue to provide the churches of the West with food for thought.

However, the era of great episcopal teachers did not last. After the period of the church fathers, which might be described as "fat years" for theology, came the "lean years", which lasted until the 12th century. As the church became more powerful, the bishops came to be more concerned with administration, canon law and their influence in society than with the teaching of theology. Charlemagne tried to put pressure on them with regard to teaching, reminding them that they had undertaken to establish schools, in suitable places, for the education of children and of the ministers of the church, a task which must not be neglected. There was little response from the bishops to this imperial advice, but luckily the monastic orders proved willing to meet this great need. Indeed most of the prominent theological teachers in the Dark Ages, until the founding of the universities, were from a monastic background, teachers such as John Scotus Erigena at Malmesbury, Rabanus Maurus at Fulda and Anselm at Bec.

We find then, for a very long period, that the church was without a class of men specifically set apart for the full-time study and teaching of theology, men who had the freedom to do this without having other responsibilities which they might have to neglect. This raises the question as to whether the church really needed such a body of *magistri*. If it had survived without them for so long, were they necessary at all for the well-being of the church?

It seems to me that an answer is to be found in church history. The church survived the period without teachers, but for much of that period it did not fulfill, or did not fulfill adequately, those of its tasks which were specifically theological; and, as Yves Congar has written, "If theologians are needed, this is not to ensure the existence of the church, but to ensure the right accomplishment of its mission."[2] For a long time the church did not advance the study of the scriptures, nor did it help its members to understand them. Further, it did not help the whole people of God to give a clear account of their faith to unbelievers, and did not consider how that faith might best be interpreted to people who were not of Graeco-Roman culture. And it did not reflect sufficiently on the constant need for reform or renewal of the church in the light of its origin.

It is obvious that these tasks could be accomplished only when men of high calibre were able to give them their undivided attention. In most cases, the bishops were quite unable to do this because of their many other responsibilities. A very few quite exceptional men, such as Augustine with his inexhaustible spiritual and mental power, could be bishop, theological teacher and theological writer at the same time. Most bishops, however, could not achieve this. This is not a criticism of bishops in general. Many of them indeed became worldly, and were in no sense teachers of their flock, but many others deserve gratitude for trying to do the impossible.

It must be asked whether it was necessary to accord to bishops such an exclusive responsibility for the transmission and interpretation of the faith that teachers became secondary figures. It might well have been better if the church had adopted the Pauline principle that leadership in the church is the responsibility of both overseers and teachers, who should thus be associated with one another in this common task.

There is, however, one serious criticism of the hierarchy which we dare not omit. This is the fact that the hierarchy did not have sufficient belief in the power of the message which they had to impart to retain the principle that no one should be coerced into faith. When heretical movements appeared in southern France in the 15th century, the papacy put pressure on the secular authorities to use violent means to suppress them. Soon afterwards, the Inquisition was established and led, in the words of the Declaration on Religious Freedom of the Second Vatican Council, to "ways of acting which were less in accord with the spirit of the gospel, and even opposed to it". Unfortunately, these "ways of acting" were based on official teaching by the church authorities of the period. The church historian Karl von Hase puts the matter bluntly: "The justifiable rule of the church, its pastoral office, became a malicious despotism, homicide in the name of Christ."[3] By formulating and defending the doctrine that it was the duty of the church to condemn heretics to death, the *magisterium* itself became heretical.

NOTES

[1] Lietzmann, *Geschichte der Alten Kirche*, II:305.
[2] Yves Congar, *Les théologiens et l'Eglise*, Quatre Fleuves, Paris, Beauchesne, 1980, p.8.
[3] Karl von Hase, *Kirchengeschichte*, Leipzig, Breitkopf & Härtel, 1877, II:376.

6. A *Magisterium* of the *Magistri?*

In 1956, Pius XII warned theologians that it would be erroneous to think of themselves as *magistri magisterii*, that is, as masters of the teaching authority.[1] There were many theologians in the later middle ages, however, who would have disagreed with him. Congar describes that period as marking "the beginning of what may be called a *magisterium* of the doctors of the church".[2] The *magistri* came to occupy a place of authority and claimed that it was their special province to decide what was the true faith. This had come about because of a strong upsurge in the demand for higher education, which the cathedral schools could not meet. From about 1200, therefore, universities were founded. Paris became the most famous theological centre and owed its reputation as the "second capital of Christendom" to the work of its theological faculty. The university theologians developed a strong professional consciousness. Using the same language, methodology and authoritative texts, they formed a strong international fraternity, deeply conscious of its status as the interpreter of the "queen of sciences".

The official theory at the time was that theological teachers received their authority to teach from the pope. The chancellor of the university granted the *licentia legendi, regendi, disputandi, docandi, in sacra theologiae facultate* with a formula beginning with the words *Auctoritate apostolica*, which is to say that the authority to teach was derived from the pope. The place of the theologians in the life of mediaeval society became so important, however, that they often spoke and acted as if they represented an independent source of authority. Pope Boniface VIII had to remind them that "it is to us that the world is entrusted, not to you".[3]

Thomas Aquinas gave a prudent answer to this question. He drew a distinction between two different types of *magisterium*: the *magisterium cathedrae pastoralis* and the *magisterium cathedrae magistralis,* the first being the *magisterium* of the hierarchy, who had jurisdiction, and the second the *magisterium* of the theologians, who had *scientia* or learning. The fact that both of these conceptions can be described as *magisterium* and that both are qualified by the word *cathedra*, meaning "seat of authority", shows how much importance Aquinas attached to the task of the theologians. It may well be that we must see in this light his refusal to accept the call to become archbishop. It would seem that he considered his service to the church as a theologian of greater urgency than the service he could have rendered as a member of the hierarchy. When he was canonized and became "the angelic doctor" of the church, he was painted preaching from a high *cathedra*, with the pope and the emperor as attentive listeners. The painter obviously believed that the teaching of Aquinas had been his most important function.

As the position of the universities became consolidated, and especially during the long period when the papacy was greatly weakened by the "Babylonian exile" and the great schism, theological faculties increasingly became centres of great authority. They formed the new generation of church leaders and served as counsellors not only to the hierarchy but also to governments. In the extremely complicated efforts to find a way out of the chaotic situation of the papacy, the universities played a leading role. It was inevitable that this would lead to tension between them and the papacy, a tension represented sometimes by two popes.

M.D. Chenu has described the position of the *magistri* at that time: "They are officially entitled to speak of faith and doctrine; they 'determine' after having discussed the problem and their solution is authorized. They are not authorities in the decisive sense of the ecclesiastical *magisterium*, for neither their historical situation nor the nature of their work implies this, but they have theological standing [*lieu*]. The theological school [*scola*] exists within the church under the Father in the faith."[4] These distinctions are so subtle that one has to be a scholastic theologian to understand them fully. It is not surprising, therefore, that there was a never-ending debate as to how far theologians should be allowed to go. There were some fairly radical points of view. For example, Godefroi de Fontaines said that the *magistri* had the right not to accept the decisions of bishops, and might give a decisive opinion on matters coming within the competence of the pope. William of Ockham, who has had a very considerable and enduring international influence, said that, since the popes of his time were only canonists, they did not understand theology and that in matters of faith it was better to follow the theologians who had real *scientia*.[5]

Jean Gerson, the famous French theologian and mystic, believed firmly in the hierarchy as the God-given structure of the church, but as chancellor of the university of Paris he was a prominent spokesman for the *magistri* and sought to combine loyalty to the hierarchical tradition with theological freedom. This can be seen from the prophetic sermon he preached before Pope Benedict XIII in Tarascon in 1404. He reminded the pope of the conflict between St Peter and St Paul described in the second chapter of the epistle to the Galatians, pointing out that, because St Peter had been wrong in a matter of faith, St Paul asked him to account for his behaviour. Gerson further suggested that, if St Peter had resisted, St Paul would have had the right to appeal to a general council of the church, which would have had authority over St Peter.[6] In this way, Gerson tried to force Benedict to resign and prepare the way for a general council to restore unity and reform the church *in capite et membris*. It is particularly noteworthy that Gerson developed his interpretation of the relationship between St Peter and St Paul by stating that there was a Pauline as well as a Petrine succession. On the basis of the second chapter of Galatians, he maintained that "the Highest Pontifex, who had succeeded Peter in the apostolate, could be publicly reproved by the theological doctor, who had succeeded Paul in the office of preaching, even when the Pontifex had not become heretical nor erred in the faith".[7] The short formula for these two successions is: *Petrus praeest principatu, Paulus pollet magistratu totius Ecclesiae*. Gerson did not want to attack the official hierarchical system, and clearly did not see that the idea of a Pauline succession parallel to the Petrine could be used to undermine that system. He did not foresee that in the following century theologians would appear who, in the name of St Paul, would raise radical questions about the structure of the church.

When at last the general councils met, the *magistri* naturally played an important role in their deliberations. In Constance in 1414 three hundred doctors were present. It is remarkable that it was a very prominent member of the hierarchy, Pierre Cardinal d'Ailly, who proposed that the doctors of theology should be allowed to vote. D'Ailly, like Gerson, was a former chancellor of the university of Paris, which had decided to claim the right to participate in the voting. His arguments must have irritated the bishops considerably. He said: "Doctors were placed on an equal level with bishops and presbyters by the apostles. Since an ignorant bishop or ruler is only a mitred or crowned ass, the doctors must sit with them, to compensate for their ignorance."[8] This proposal was accepted in a modified form. The voting was by nations and, within the national delegations, the *magistri* could vote. It is evident that the theologians played a particularly important role in convincing the participants that they should solemnly proclaim the principle that the pope was subject to a council of the whole church.

At the next general council, held in Basel in 1431, doctors of theology were again strongly represented. The council formed four "deputations" or sections to deal with the different issues on the agenda, and in each of these theologians took a prominent part. In the early stages of the council good progress was made, but the papacy had regained sufficient strength to enable it to resist those who defended the conciliarist policy.

There came a day in 1439 when three hundred doctors were in session with thirteen priests and seven bishops. The great days of conciliarism were over, but teachers of theology had not yet lost their influence. It is striking to discover that in the 16th and 17th centuries the universities were still being consulted as centres of authority on fundamental problems. A famous example is provided by the consultation of the universities about the divorce of Henry VIII. When the king had failed to obtain from the pope a declaration that his marriage to Catherine of Aragon was invalid, Dr Thomas Cranmer, a Cambridge theologian, suggested that the quickest way to decide the question was to consult the universities. He said: "There is but one truth in it, which no men ought or better can discuss than the divines."[9] The majority of the universities decided in Henry's favour. We find an echo of this international debate in Shakespeare's *Henry VIII* where it is said that the opinions of Cranmer

> Have satisfied the king for his divorce,
> Together with all famous colleges
> Almost in Christendom.[10]

Another example of the influence of the universities is their consultation about the controversy between Martin Luther and Johannes Eck. In 1519 at Leipzig, during the academic debate between the two professors, it was agreed that the universities of Paris and Erfurt should be asked to be the arbiters of the contest, and to adjudge the victory. Luther had been impressed by the writings of d'Ailly and Gerson, and had therefore hoped that his point of view would be understood and approved in Paris. However, the university of Erfurt was unwilling to commit itself, and the doctors in Paris, after considering the matter for some time, condemned Luther's position on the basis of his *De Captivitate Babylonica*. The theological faculties of Louvain and Cologne also condemned some of the theses of Luther.

It is important to ask whether the academic *magistri* who for three centuries had filled an important place in the church had made a strong positive contribution to its life. Had they really been the *cathedra et thronum fidei*, the words with which Gerson had described the university of Paris? In the opinion of the most prominent representatives of the 16th century, it would seem that they had done more harm than good. Erasmus and Luther disagreed on many points, but on this issue they were in accord. In the chapter on theologians in his *In Praise of Folly*, Erasmus in his sarcasm seems to express indignation rather than amusement.

"They regard themselves as almost the equal of gods whenever they are greeted with holy respectfulness as 'Magister noster', and they feel that in that name is found something of the quality attached to the word the Jews may not mention." Luther spoke of the "shameful pride and ambition in theology which is the source of all evil and a consuming fire".[11] Both condemned the hair splitting of scholastic teachers. "That is why I hate the opinions of the Thomists and Scotists and other famous professors," said Luther.[12] The *magistri* had shown an amazing lack of proportion in spending a great deal of time and energy on the discussion of problems which were unimportant, or even totally artificial. They had neglected their task of calling the church back to its original source, holy scripture, which has to be reinterpreted to each new age, and in the light of which the church has to look critically at its own life, so that it may be purified and renewed. In two ways, however, the *magistri* had rendered an important and much needed service. They had shown concern for the unity of the church in their attempts to heal the great schism, and they had supported the principle that the church is a place not of monologue, but of dialogue. The real issue at the time of the two 15th-century councils was not the question of the most appropriate structure for the church, as most of the canonists believed, but the deeper question as to whether power in the church would be responsible power, that is, power which could justify its decisions in the light of the revelation given to the whole people of God. This vital question was not solved, and would continue to occupy the church for a long time. Similarly, no clear decision was reached about the place of the *magistri* in the church's life.

NOTES

[1] Quoted in Congar, *Les théologiens et l'Eglise*, p.115.
[2] Yves Congar, "Le magistère et les docteurs", in *Revue des sciences philosophiques et théologiques*, 1976, p.104.
[3] Barbara Tuchman, *A Distant Mirror*, New York, Knopf, 1978, p.22.
[4] Quoted in G.H.M. Posthumus Meyjes, *Jean Gerson*, The Hague, M. Nijhoff, 1963, p.268.
[5] Posthumus Meyjes, *Kerkhistorische Studien*, 1982, pp.525-26.
[6] Posthumus Meyjes, *Jean Gerson*, p.95.
[7] *Ibid.*, p.269.
[8] Von Hase, *Kirchengeschichte*, II: 337.
[9] C. Sydney Carter, *The English Church and the Reformation*, London, Longmans, Green, 1925, p.45.
[10] William Shakespeare, *Henry VIII*, Act 3, Scene 2.
[11] Martin Luther, *Tischreden*, Reclam, p.232.
[12] Rudolf Thiel, *Luther*, Vienna, Neff, 1986, p.205.

7. *Magistri* as Reformers

When Vladimir Soloviev elaborated his vision of the reunion of the three main branches of Christianity as the eschatological conclusion of world history, he imagined a meeting in Jerusalem of a pope called Peter, a *starets* or saintly monk called John and a certain Professor Pauli. The choice of the first two characters to represent Roman Catholicism and Orthodoxy was obvious, but it may be asked whether it was right to characterize the Protestant churches as churches dominated by academic teachers in the tradition of St Paul.

It is true that nearly all the leaders of the movements that prepared the way for the Reformation, and those of the Reformation itself, were theologians with university training and many of them were professors of theology. John Wycliffe was master of Balliol College, Oxford, and held the degree of doctor of divinity. For a number of years the university allowed him to teach his radical ideas which called into question the whole hierarchical system. Finally, however, under strong pressure from the papacy and from the archbishop of Canterbury, the university authorities had to condemn him and the university was placed under strict ecclesiastical control. Among the Lollards who avidly read his translation of the Bible, on the other hand, Wycliffe continued to be revered as the "evangelical doctor". John Hus, at one time rector of the university of Prague, was known as Magister Hus. When the council of Constance had condemned him to death, he signed one of his last letters "Magister John Hus, in chains and in prison, already at the border of the life beyond".[1] It must have been a severe shock to him to find that among the most aggressive spokesmen of the party demanding his condemnation were some of his colleagues, *magistri*, and leading lights of the Sorbonne, such as Pierre d'Ailly and Jean Gerson, from whom he had surely expected an attitude of understanding and sympathy.

The setting of Martin Luther's life was entirely academic from 1501, when he became a student at the University of Erfurt, until 1517 when he published his famous Ninety-five Theses. He obtained degrees in the faculties of law and theology, began to teach in 1509 and received the degree of *magister* of sacred theology in 1512. By that time he was also doctor of sacred scripture and began to give exegetical lectures on the Psalms, the epistle to the Romans and the epistle to the Galatians. In 1517, when he felt bound to protest against the evils of the traffic in indulgences, he posted his theses in Latin on the door of the castle church in Wittenberg, intending them to lead to an academic debate. He described himself therefore as "Reverend Father Martin Luther, Magister of Arts, Master of Sacred Theology and Teacher Therein". There was no immediate reaction from the universities, but the theses were translated into the vernacular and thus became widely known in non-academic circles. The debate between Luther and Johannes Eck in Leipzig in 1519 was, however, again a purely academic affair, surrounded by all the complicated ceremonies of academic tradition; and throughout his life Luther continued, in spite of his many other responsibilities, to be a university teacher.

Luther's close collaborator and friend, Philipp Melanchthon, was a scholar of exceptional brilliance. *Magister* at twelve years of age, he became professor at Wittenberg in 1518 when he was twenty-one. For his knowledge of Hebrew, Greek and Latin, of philosophy and theology, he was called the *praeceptor Germaniae*.

Calvin spent his years of study in three faculties. He first studied law, then switched to the faculty of letters. When he published his commentary on Seneca it was clear that his aim was to become a teacher in that faculty. He then became convinced that God wanted him to go "in another direction" and he began to study theology. He wrote a sermon for All Saints' Day for the rector of the University of Paris which was so clearly evangelical that he had to leave France. There was no university in Geneva when Calvin arrived there, and he received the title of *lecteur de l'Evangile*. His wish that Geneva should have an academy of its own was fulfilled in 1559. The first rector was Théodore de Bèze, or Beza, who had been professor of Greek in Lausanne and who became Calvin's successor in the church of Geneva.

Martin Bucer, the Strasbourg reformer, was a professor at Cambridge; Oecolampadius, the Basel reformer, taught in the faculty of theology in that city, while Thomas Cranmer was a fellow of Jesus College, Cambridge.

All this may seem to show that the Reformation was essentially an academic affair, a sort of conspiracy of professional theologians, so that it is correct to regard Reformed churches as churches created and dominated by professors. I admit that this is the first impression received, but on further consideration we find that it is misleading. These professors did not live academic lives and their original ambition, to live between the study and the classroom, devoting all their energies to writing and teaching, was not fulfilled. Their careers were deflected as they accepted responsibility for action in the life of the church and society. The *magistri* considered these men as a blot on the profession – for one thing, self-respecting *magistri* wrote all their works in Latin and not in French, German or English.

It was not without reluctance that the Reformers left their ivory towers. Luther confessed again and again that he would have liked to keep quiet, but was constantly pushed into the midst of alarms. He said: "God does not lead me but he both draws and pursues me. I am not master of my own life" *(Ich bin meiner selbst nicht mächtig)*. When his first writings in German received an enthusiastic reception, he said: "What I have done happens under compulsion; I am always ready to remain silent, if they will only not force the gospel to be silent."[2] Calvin spoke a similar language in the preface to his *Commentary on the Psalms*, one of the very few autobiographical reflections we have of him. To make his meaning clear, I am giving here a translation which remains very close to the original. Calvin wrote: "Although my purpose had always been to live in privacy and without being known, God has led me in such a way and turned me around with such changes of direction that he has never allowed me to rest in any place, until in spite of my natural inclination he has put me in the glare [of public life] and, as the saying goes, forced me to enter the game" *(venir en jeu)*. Calvin was referring here specifically to the hard decision he had taken to give up the dream of a quiet, scholarly life. He described his meeting with Guillaume Farel, who was seeking his help in the reformation of the Genevan church: "After having heard that I had some special study projects for which I wanted to reserve my freedom, and seeing that he was getting nowhere with his requests, he went so far as to utter an imprecation that it might please God to curse my quiet life and the tranquillity of studies which I desired, if in a situation of such great need I should turn away and refuse to give help and support."

The Reformers and the professors who represented the new humanist spirit had in common a desire to return to the sources. Erasmus and Melanchthon both made strong pleas for the study of Greek and Hebrew so that the source of the faith could be rediscovered. Melanchthon defined Luther's life-work as guiding men to the sources, and Calvin explained to Sadolet that he wanted to bring Christianity back to its original purity. There is, however, a fundamental difference. For scholars the source, in this case the Bible, was primarily a source of knowledge, while for the Reformers it was a source of transforming power. Luther said: *Sermo enim Dei venit mutaturus et innovaturus mundum, quoties venit* [whenever the word of God comes, it comes to renew and transform the world]. The word of God is the one and only authority.

All teaching and preaching in the church have to be judged by this criterion. No teacher, no bishop, no pope, nobody, can claim that because of his position he is not submitted to it. There can be no exemption. It is for this reason that Luther found that, of all principles contained in canon law, the most objectionable was that "the first see shall not be judged by anyone".[3]

The *magisterium* is the right and duty of the whole church. Who then has authority to teach? In 1523, Luther entitled one of his works "That a Christian Congregation [*Versammlung*] or Church [*Gemeinde*] has the Right and Power to Make Judgments Concerning Doctrine and to Call Teachers, to Install Them and to Dismiss Them". If a Christian church is one where the word of God is clearly preached, that would seem to mean that the preachers, and more particularly the teachers of the preachers, become the true *magisterium*. Teachers and preachers are, however, not the masters of the word of God but its servants, so that not only must their words faithfully reflect the revelation in holy scripture, but they must also accept that the church, guided by the Holy Spirit, can decide whether their teaching is true to the faith. In this connection, Luther and other Reformers often quoted the tenth chapter of the gospel of St John: "The sheep follow the Shepherd, for they know his voice." From this text Luther drew the conclusion that "the sheep should judge whether they [the teachers] teach with the voice of Christ or with the voice of a stranger".

He applied the same criterion to the ecumenical councils, believing that the early councils had indeed defended biblical faith. He further declared that he would be ready to participate in a council which would purify the church, provided it was a gathering of "men who are solid scholars of holy scripture"[4] but he had little hope that such a council would meet in his life-time.

Luther's conception of the *magisterium* is therefore in principle that of a dialogue between teachers and church members. Such a dialogue can however be realized only if each of the two parties is able to offer the other that mutual correction which characterizes Christian fellowship. Owing to the complicated circumstances in which he found himself, Luther was not able to establish a church order which clearly laid down how church members should be represented. As it was not established how one party to the dialogue, the church members, should function, the other, that is, the teachers, became the dominating factor in the situation.

Thus, in spite of the original intention of its founder, the Lutheran church became a church in which theologians exercised a de facto *magisterium*. As the Lutheran representatives on the mixed Roman

Catholic/Lutheran commission of 1981 stated in their report, the elaboration of doctrine in Lutheranism had come to be primarily the task of
theological faculties.[5] In the Reformed churches, there is the same
emphasis on the authority of scripture, but in one important aspect
Calvin went further than Luther. He was convinced that holy scripture
contains definite instructions for the establishment of a correct church
order. Thus the "Ordonnances ecclésiastiques de Genève" of 1561 set
forth "le gouvernement spirituel, tel que notre Seigneur a demontré et
institué par sa Parole" [spiritual government, as our Lord demonstrated
it and instituted it by his word]. Calvin's *Institutes* and the various confessions of the Reformed churches teach that *politeia* or church government based on the word of God[6] must comprise several orders: ministers
(sometimes subdivided into pastors and doctors), presbyters or elders
and deacons. In principle these were on an equal footing and there was
no hierarchy. It was their duty constantly to apply that mutual correction
which ensures that no one seeks to take the place of the one true Head of
the church, and that all fulfill their function as members of the body. The
magister is, however, mentioned in several of the confessional documents. The second Helvetic confession of 1566 says simply: "The doctors give instruction and teach the true faith and piety." The church order
adopted by the synod of Dordrecht in 1619 states: "The office of doctors
and professors of theology is to interpret holy scripture and to maintain
pure doctrine against heresy and error" (for other examples see ch. 15).

This new approach to the problem of the place of the *magistri*
seemed hopeful, as it could have led to fruitful dialogue between theologians and leaders of the church, including elders representing the
laity. Unfortunately, at the very moment when such a relationship of true
conciliarity had been defined, there occurred an event which discredited
theology in the eyes of many both inside and outside the Reformed
churches for a long time to come. The occasion was the synod of Dordrecht, held in 1618-19. The synod had been summoned to deal with
matters pertaining to the Netherlands Reformed Church. It was attended,
however, by a considerable number of theologians and other church
leaders sent from abroad by their governments; from Great Britain, for
example, came a representative of King James I. These visitors were not
only present as observers, but also played an important part in the discussions. The central issue was the correct interpretation of the doctrine
of predestination. At the university of Leyden, then in its early years,
were two professors, Arminius and Gomarus, who held different conceptions of this doctrine and each taught his own. There were strength
and weakness in both positions. Arminius had a tendency towards Pela-
gianism, while his opponent speculated about the will of God as if any-

thing could be known about it apart from the revelation in Christ. Both professors found followers who became their passionate defenders and the controversy became a major political issue. This was a moment at which the church could have displayed a truly Christian *magisterium* in bringing the parties together in a fraternal dialogue in an ecumenical setting. Sadly, this opportunity was missed – worse than that, the synod, instead of encouraging dialogue, acted from the start as a tribunal and treated the Arminians or Remonstrants, as they were also called, as the accused. These were not given sufficient chance to defend themselves, and the outcome was their excommunication. The Scottish theologian Dr Balcanqual, a convinced Calvinist, reported in a letter to the ambassador of his country in The Hague: "No ancient church and no reformed church has ever proposed so many articles of faith to be held in order to avoid excommunication."[7]

There seem to me to have been three reasons for this debacle. First, at that time theologians used *disputatio*, the style and technique of debating societies for theological discussions. It was not understood that the *koinonia* of which the New Testament speaks requires dialogue for mutual edification. Secondly, theologians had not freed themselves from the speculations of the schoolmen, who had attempted to explain all mysteries. Thirdly, the synod was deeply influenced by politicians who desired uniformity of belief and therefore did not permit true religious liberty.

NOTES

[1] Richard Friedenthal, *Ketzer und Rebell*, Munich, R. Piper, 1972, pp.156,172.
[2] Thiel, *Luther*, pp.290,319.
[3] "Warum des Pabst und seiner Jünger Bücher von Dr. Martin Luther verbrannt sind".
[4] Martin Luther, *Von den Konzilien und Kirchen* (1539).
[5] Secrétariat pour l'Unité des Chrétiens: *Service d'information*, 1982/1.
[6] Confessio Belgica XXX.
[7] *Korte Historie Synode van Dordrecht*, 1671, p.320.

8. The *Magisterium* in the Context of Papal Infallibility

The council of Trent (1545-63) answered many of the questions which had been raised by the Reformers, but did not provide a precise definition of the *magisterium*. The old question as to whether the ultimate authority rested with ecumenical councils or was to be found in the dogmatic decision of the pope remained a debatable issue. In 1682, a convention consisting of eight archbishops, twenty-six bishops and thirty-eight other clergy met in Paris and adopted the Déclaration du Clergé de France. This stated that the decrees of the council of Constance respecting the authority of general councils could not be challenged, and that the judgment of the pope, unless it had received the assent of the church, was not incapable of correction. Bishop Jacques Bossuet, an indefatigable fighter for what he considered to be genuine, ancient tradition, defended this Gallican declaration with great vigour. His thesis, based on the writings of the church fathers and other theologians, was that the pope is not infallible in his decisions or doctrines of the faith.[1] One churchman whose words he quoted was Pope Hadrian VI who, when still professor in Louvain, had expressed the certainty that popes were fallible even in matters of the faith. Bossuet also expressed full agreement with the profession of faith set out by Pius IV: "I recognize that the Roman church is holy, catholic and apostolic, that she is the mother and mistress of all churches, and I promise and swear true obedience to the pope, successor of St Peter, Prince of the Apostles and Vicar of Jesus Christ." At the same time, Bossuet held that the church had to continue to follow the Vincentian canon ("We believe that which has been believed everywhere and always") rather than "what the pope alone has decided".[2]

It is very striking that the great traditionalist Bossuet defended his Gallican position by very frequent references to the theologians of the University of Paris. His argument was not based on decisions of the French hierarchy but on sources which he referred to as "les sentiments des docteurs de Paris", "de la faculté de théologie de Paris", "de l'école de Paris", "la doctrine de l'université" or "la doctrine de la Faculté".[3] The impression gained is that, when the Sorbonne had spoken, that was for Bossuet *causa finita*.

The Gallican resistance of the French church against Rome collapsed when Louis XIV arrived at a compromise with the pope. The official Gallican resistance was at an end, but there nevertheless always remained a remnant of support for the Gallican position. During the reign of Charles X (1824-30), the government requested the bishops to sign the "Déclaration" of 1682. Most of them refused, but there were fourteen among them who were willing to sign.

The 19th century was a time of sharp ideological polarization. On the one hand there was a strong demand for emancipation in political and social life which found expression in the revolutionary movements of 1830, 1848 and 1870. There was, however, at the same time a strong anti-revolutionary trend, which expressed itself in the holy alliance, in romantic dreams of a return to the past and in authoritarian politics. Many anti-revolutionary thinkers considered a strongly centralized infallible papacy essential to avoid a disintegration of society. Ultramontanism was therefore at one and the same time a religious conviction and a political ideology. Joseph de Maistre's book *Du pape* uses both political and theological arguments. Later, Louis Veuillot, a layman who attacked liberalism in all its forms and who was a fanatical believer in the doctrine of infallibility, became what a biographer of Pius IX called "l'enfant chéri" of the pope.[4] Many theologians, however, continued to seek to reconcile theology and modern thought. In 1863, Dr Johann Döllinger, an outstanding professor at the University of Munich, called together a conference of Roman Catholic scholars and gave an opening address which has been characterized as "a declaration of the rights of theology". Stating that Germany was called to be the torch-bearer of Roman Catholic theology, he pointed out that it could flourish only in an atmosphere of freedom. Just as in the Old Testament there were not only priests but also prophets, so there was in the church, in addition to the hierarchical power, an extraordinary power which was the science of theology. Theology exerted its influence through public opinion and in the long run all, even the leaders of the church, must accept its findings. Neo-scholasticism was an antiquated system, which was incapable of responding to the questions posed in the modern world.

The Vatican reacted vigorously to Döllinger's statement. In a *Breve* to the archbishop of Munich it was declared intolerable that theologians should meet without permission from the hierarchy whose task it was to direct and supervise them. The theologians in question had failed to show the obedience they owed to the *magisterium ecclesiae*. Scholars were expected to submit not only in matters declared by the infallible judgment of the church to be a dogma of the faith, but also to the decisions of the *magisterium*, of the Roman congregations, and the common teaching of the theologians.[5]

In 1864, the Vatican issued the "Syllabus of Errors", a catalogue of eighty modern ideas which it considered to be wrong. Several of the criticisms included in the syllabus were clearly addressed to the German theologians and those in other countries who might be tempted to follow their lead. The syllabus condemned for instance the belief, held by the Vatican to be erroneous, "that the method and principles by which the old scholastic doctors cultivated theology are no longer suitable to the demands of this age", and the further belief "that the Roman pontiff can, and ought to, reconcile himself to, and agree with, progress, liberalism and modern civilization".

Conservative forces in the church became increasingly convinced that the advance of modern ideas, dangerous in their view, should be met by the strongest possible reaffirmation of papal authority. A campaign was therefore launched to bring about the solemn proclamation of the infallibility of the pope. At first it was hoped that this could be achieved by acclamation, but this proved to be impossible because a considerable number of bishops resisted the idea. In 1868 therefore Pope Pius IX convoked an ecumenical council to be held in Rome. It was not announced in advance that the doctrine of infallibility would be on the agenda, but it soon became clear from various publications that in fact, as the archbishop of Paris Monsignor Georges Darboy put it, "infallibility was not one of the reasons for the council, it was the sole reason". Opposition proved stronger than had been expected. Some bishops did not actually oppose the doctrine, but felt that it was not the moment to proclaim it, as it would increase the estrangement between the church and modern life. There were others who thought that a belief in the infallibility of the pope was a misinterpretation of the true tradition of the infallibility of the church, and it was therefore wrong to teach this. In the light of history it was not surprising that one of the centres of opposition to the new dogma was Paris. The archbishop of Paris stated firmly that he was against this attempt by the Ultramontanist party to magnify papal power, and the dean of the faculty of theology at the Sorbonne, Henri Maret, the titular bishop of Sura, made it clear that the "sentiments de l'Ecole de Paris" were still alive. In his book *Du concile général et de la paix religieuse*, which appeared a few weeks before the opening of the council, he maintained that the Gallican ecclesiology expressed a truth which was of eternal value. As for Germany, Döllinger also published a book, *Der Papst und das Konzil*, in which he demonstrated that there was no historical justification for the proposed dogma.

The preparatory work for the council was in the hands of a group of theologians known as the Roman school, who were for the most part Jesuits who defended neo-scholasticism. Very few theologians of other tendencies were invited to assist in these preparations, and those who were not Vatican insiders had little chance to make a contribution. One of them, the very learned Prof. Karl Hefel, said that he did not know why he had come to Rome.

When the council opened, it became clear that there was a deep divergence of opinion among the bishops. Numerically, there was a large majority in favour of papal infallibility, but the minority included the bishops of some of the main historical centres of Roman Catholicism, and the tale of the tremendous pressure exerted on them is a dark page in church history. Pope Pius IX himself used all possible means to intimidate the recalcitrant bishops, showing no respect for their convictions. It seems that he did, in fact, utter his famous words to Cardinal Guidi, who was underlining the discrepancy between the new dogma and tradition: "La tradizione sono io" [I am the tradition].

This situation obviously favoured a positive decision on the acceptance of the dogma. The preliminary voting on the "Constitutio" was 451 *placet* (for), 88 *non placet* (against) and 62 *placet juxta modum* (for, with amendments). The final vote was limited to *placet* and *non placet*. However, almost all those bishops who were against the motion left Rome before the vote, so that in the end the dogma was accepted with only two opposing votes.

The dogma states that the pope, speaking *ex cathedra*, that is, in his capacity as pastor and teacher of all Christians, when defining on his supreme apostolic authority, through the divine assistance promised him in blessed Peter, a doctrine of faith or morals to be held by the universal church, is endowed with that infallibility with which the Divine Redeemer has willed that his church should be equipped when defining doctrine concerning faith or morals. Therefore definitions laid down by the Roman pontiff, even when he is speaking on his own authority without the consent of the church, cannot be changed *(ex sese, non autem ex consensu ecclesiae)*.

Yves Congar draws attention to the fact, clearly stated in the council, that infallibility is here presented as an attribute of the primacy. Bishop Gasser had said: "We derive from the primacy the supreme power to teach"; according to Congar this was a reminder that the council was held at a time when the social and political climate was one of restoration, of opposition to liberation movements and of a maximum reaffirmation of authority.[6] The definition, which was the outcome of a long, extremely complicated and at times heated discussion, was intended to provide a conclusive answer to the question of the nature of the *magisterium*. There remained, however, several problems of interpretation which had not been settled. Did the pope speak *ex cathedra* only when he solemnly proclaimed a new dogma, or also when he took a definite stand on a question of faith or morals by means of an encyclical? Was *ex sese, non autem ex consensu ecclesiae* simply a rejection of the Gallican position that the pope was infallible only when acting together with a council, or did it give him freedom to teach doctrine as truth without having consulted the church?

After some hesitation almost all the bishops who had opposed the dogma at the council submitted to the pope. A number of theological professors, however, refused to accept the council's decision. In 1871, a congress was held in Munich at which the leadership was provided by university teachers. These Old Catholics, as they came to be called, declared that they remained faithful to traditional teaching and rejected the doctrines of the infallibility of the pope and of his universal jurisdiction. They stated that the laity, the clergy and the study of theology all had the right to witness and to be heard when decisions on the faith were made. At a second congress, in Cologne in 1872, the Old Catholics decided independently to choose a bishop, and Dr Joseph Reinkens, professor of theology in Breslau, was consecrated by the bishop of Deventer, a bishop of the Dutch Jansenist communion. The Old Catholics never became a large church, but they maintained a theological tradition of high quality and became pioneers in the ecumenical movement.[7]

NOTES

[1] Jacques Bossuet, *Abrégé de la défense de la déclaration*, 1814 ed., p.331.
[2] *Ibid.*, p.48.
[3] *Ibid.*, pp.253,401,243,245,395,88,250,424.
[4] Fernand Hayward, *Pie IX et son temps*, Paris, Plon, 1948, p.154.
[5] Joseph Hoffmann, *Les théologiens et l'Eglise*, p.92; and von Hase, *Kirchengeschichte*, p.923.
[6] *Revue des sciences philosophiques et théologiques*, 1976, p.108.
[7] *Internationale Kirchliche Zeitschrift*.

9. The Threat of Divorce between the *Magistri* and the *Magisterium*

In the years after the First Vatican Council, Roman Catholic theologians were in a difficult position. They had been told by the pope that their "most noble task was to show how doctrine was to be found in the sources of revelation, as defined by the church".[1] This seemed to reduce all theology to the level of that described as "Denzinger theology", from the name of the collected edition of official teachings. It should be remembered that this was said precisely at the time when, in churches other than the Roman Catholic Church, much valuable work was being done in theology and developments in the study of history were forcing theologians to face many new problems.

To understand the significance of the modernist movement in theology, it is best to consider the early part of the 20th century. Modernism had become a controversial issue in the Protestant churches already in the final decades of the 19th century, and had led in some cases to disciplinary action. In the Anglican church, John William Colenso, the bishop of Natal, aroused strong protests when, in his commentary on the epistle to the Romans, he denied that there could be eternal punishment, and when in further writings he challenged the traditional authority and accuracy of the Pentateuch and the book of Joshua. In the United States Charles Briggs, at one time professor at the Union Theological Seminary, and in Scotland William Robertson Smith, caused dismay and dissension by their higher criticism of the Old Testament. In the Lutheran church, disagreement arose about the validity of the Apostles' Creed, a dispute which was known as the *Apostolikumstreit*.

It was, however, in the first decade of the new century that modernism became what the encyclical *Pascendi Gregis* described as a tidal wave and a critical problem in the Roman Catholic Church as well as in the Protestant churches. Every year brought new challenges to traditional theology. In 1900, Harnack's lectures on *Das Wesen des Christentums*[2] had an unprecedented success, running into seven editions in German, with translation into fifteen languages. In these lectures he declared that the essence of Christianity is not the message about Christ, but Christ's message to man concerning God's fatherhood and his kingdom.

The next year brought William Wrede's book on the messianic secret, which sought to show that the gospel according to St Mark presents a very biased picture of Jesus. In 1902, Alfred Loisy published *L'Evangile et l'Eglise*, conceived as a Catholic answer to Harnack but considered by the Roman Catholic authorities as a dangerous book because the author used the same historical and critical method as Harnack. The same year saw Hermann Gunkel's introduction of the concept of *Gattungsgeschichte*, which later became known as form criticism and had very far-reaching consequences for the interpretation of the Bible. There was also the start of the great battle about *Bibel und Babel*, launched by those who saw in the religion of Israel a sub-division of Babylonian religion. At the same time, Ernst Troeltsch raised the question as to whether the Christian revelation was absolute,[3] and William James' famous book *Varieties of Religious Experience* appeared.

In 1903, a handbook on the history of religion was published. Started by Cornelis Tiele and completed by Nathan Söderblom, it provided a wealth of information on the non-Christian religions, which was augmented in 1906 with the publication of James Frazer's *Golden Bough*. In that year the School of the History of Religion[4] found a leader in Wilhelm Bossuet, who wrote *Das Wesen der Religion*. It was also in 1903 that Loisy published his monumental work on the gospel of St John, interpreting it as metahistorical rather than historical. In England George Tyrrell, a Jesuit theologian who had left the order, published *The Church and the Future* in which he rejected the authoritarian conception of the *magisterium* held by the Vatican and pleaded for spiritual freedom.

In 1904, the association "Freunde der christlichen Welt" was formed in Germany. It brought the liberal theologians together and stood for the unconditional freedom of theology, including freedom for those preparing to become pastors and teachers to form their own convictions. In the following year, the novel *Il Santo* (The Saint) by the Italian author Antonio Fogazzaro became a best-seller in several languages. Its hero is a layman who seeks to free the church from the sins of insincerity, lust for power and worldliness. It was promptly put on the Vatican Index.

Albert Schweitzer published *From Reimarus to Wrede* in 1906. In this work, he radically criticized liberal interpretation concerning Jesus on the grounds that our Lord's life and message were dominated by an eschatology which had become entirely out of date. In the same year, the Italian professor of church history, Ernesto Buonaiuti, was dismissed from his chair for having written articles with a modernistic tendency.

The decade continued to be marked by the struggle of liberal theologians. In 1907, Walter Rauschenbusch published *Christianity and the Social Crisis*. He became one of the most influential interpreters in Amer-

ica of German liberal theology and a pioneer in the Social Gospel movement. The Vatican then struck back. That very year a decree of the holy
office condemned 65 theses considered to contain modernistic teaching,
and a little later in 1907, the very long encyclical *Pascendi Gregis* was
issued, presenting a detailed analysis of modernism and condemning it in
the strongest possible terms. In the following year, Alfred Loisy was
excommunicated. On the modernist side, Tyrrell published *Christianity
at the Crossroads*. In 1910, the Vatican decided that all Roman Catholic
teachers and priests should swear an anti-modernist oath, declaring that
they accepted all and everything that had been put forward by the infallible teaching authority of the church, in particular those teachings which
were "in clear opposition to the erroneous ideas of the present time".

In 1912 a collection of essays entitled *Foundations* was published
under the general editorship of B.H. Streeter, with William Temple as
one of the contributors. Streeter himself made a strong plea for freedom
of thought and teaching, and suggested that the appearances of Christ
after his resurrection were in the nature of visions. Also in 1912 Ernst
Troeltsch's magnum opus, *Die Soziallehren der christlichen Kirchen und
Gruppen* was published. It showed that the development of relations
between church and society could be understood only by studying both
the influence of Christian ideas upon society and the influence of social
and economic conditions upon Christian thought.

It is clear from this short and very incomplete survey that the authorities of the Roman Catholic Church had had to react – in fact, they over-
reacted. No attempt was made to analyze the thought of theologians sus-
pected of modernism. No distinction was made between those who tried
loyally to fit their Catholic belief into the new intellectual pattern (as did
the Catholic layman Baron Friedrich von Hügel, who wrote that he was
"trying to make the old church as inhabitable intellectually as ever I
can"[5]) and those who simply lost their faith as a result of their historical
studies. The encyclical of 1907, *Pascendi Gregis*, is a disconcerting document. Clearly it was written in a state of panic, so instead of offering a
pastoral word of warning that there were limits to freedom in theology,
it descended to crude polemics quite unworthy of the *magisterium* of a
great church. It attempted to prove that there was a vast conspiracy to
undermine the Roman Catholic Church, and claimed that this conspiracy
was based on a theological system which denied the basic tenets of
Roman Catholicism.

There was clearly no such conspiracy, except in the imagination of
the holy office. There were individual modernists, but there was no modernist movement. There was no system, for the modernists were in the
main people who desired to share in the great task of historical research

concerning the Bible and the history of the church, which had become the focus of attention in the academic world.

The encyclical claimed that these men were working inside the church to bring about its ruin, that they were purposely mutilating history and had created by their audacity and imprudence an atmosphere of corruption which spread like an infection. Their errors were rooted in curiosity and pride, and bishops must therefore eliminate them from their positions in the church.

If this picture is compared with the impression actually made by the lives and writings of the modernists, it is hard to believe the same people are in question. Loisy had written his answer to Harnack because he wanted to show that the Roman Catholic Church was not just a remnant of the past. Fogazzaro's novel *Il Santo* was so ardently Catholic that three of the main women characters became converts to the Roman Catholic faith. Baron von Hügel, a friend of the modernists, was a sincere apologist for the Roman Catholic Church, while Ernesto Buonaiuti, whom I met several times, was not an iconoclast or an ecclesiastic revolutionary but a man who conceived historical studies to be his calling and had too much intellectual and moral integrity to repudiate his findings.

As a result of the encyclical, theology was forbidden to fulfill its creative and critical function. As H.J. Pottmeyer put it: "Since theology was condemned to have no relation to reality and to the world, it was impossible for [the theologian] to participate effectively and as a dynamic factor in the intellectual discussions of the time. It was a theology estranged from the world, which contributed to the creation of a ghetto mentality in the church, and which itself reflected that mentality."[6]

The situation was different in the Reformation churches because modernism had come to be the dominating tendency in theological faculties. As Ernst Troeltsch put it, the result was that history and Christian doctrine became separate areas of study in such a way that historical and critical studies developed into an increasingly powerful river, while doctrinal and ethical studies shrank to a thin little stream. In his great work *The History of Christian Doctrine*, Harnack stated his conclusion that the history of Christian doctrine had come to an end, because dogmatic developments in the Roman Catholic Church had reached their climax, and because any consistent consideration of Luther's Reformation would lead to the emancipation of the Protestant churches from authoritative articles of faith, that is, from dogma in the traditional sense. It was clear that in Harnack's view there could be no *magisterium* in the life of the church.[7]

Even more than Harnack, Ernst Troeltsch, with his encyclopaedic knowledge and penetrating mind, became the leading theologian of his time. He also believed that the historical approach to religion adopted by modern theology would lead inevitably to a surrendering of the absoluteness of Christianity. He said that one could speak of a Christian community inspired by Jesus as a prophet and an example, but that the idea that Jesus was the centre of the world, or even of the history of humanity, had to be given up. Further, it was possible to believe that Christianity would be among the forces which would ultimately be victorious, but that did not mean that the church should be understood as having been founded by Christ as the only place in which salvation could be found.[8]

Shortly before the first world war, the massive volumes of the encyclopaedia *Religion in Geschichte und Gegenwart* appeared, summarizing the developments in theology which had taken place in the decades just past and their results. The article on the concept of the church was written by Troeltsch. As the almost completely pluralistic type of Christian community which he advocated was entirely different from what had traditionally been known as "the church", he suggested that the word "church" should no longer be used.

There were of course a considerable number of groups and movements in the Reformation churches which were deeply alarmed by these new ideas. In general, however, they found themselves taking a defensive attitude. It was no longer possible to maintain an effective teaching authority. In most churches the old confessions of faith were still the official basis for teaching and preaching. Many church members, quite unable to understand the theological debate raging in academic circles, expected church leaders to maintain the traditional standards in presenting the faith. This put the church leaders in a very difficult position as it had become practically impossible to enforce the old rules.

We find therefore that in this period the tendency in Roman Catholicism was towards a *magisterium* which left no room for the activity of the *magistri*, while the opposite tendency appeared in the Reformation churches, that is, a domination of the *magistri* in the form of theological individualism, which left no place for a *magisterium* in any shape or form.

NOTES

[1] Pius IX, quoted in *Les théologiens et l'Eglise*, p.97.
[2] In English, *What Is Christianity?*
[3] Ernst Troeltsch, *Die Absolutheit des Christentums und die Religionsgeschichte*, Tübingen, Mohr, 1929.
[4] *Die Religionsgeschichtliche Schule.*
[5] Friedrich von Hügel, *Letters to a Niece*, London, Dent, 1929, p.165.
[6] Quoted in *Les théologiens et l'Eglise*, p.101.
[7] Adolf von Harnack, *Dogmengeschichte*, Tübingen, Mohr, 1922, pp.4,6,468.
[8] Ernst Troeltsch, *Gesammelte Schriften*, Tübingen, Mohr, 1912-25, II: 848.

10. Theologians Rediscover the Church

In the years just after the first world war, it was not clear what direction general theological development would take. Under the influence of a wave of social idealism and a belief in unlimited progress, theology in the United States of America and to some degree in the United Kingdom moved towards liberalism. In Germany, however, theology became more conservative as a result of a nostalgic defence of national traditions in a seemingly hostile world. The sharp confrontation between the theology of the social gospel and the theology centred on the world to come, which occurred at the world conference on Life and Work in 1925, did not arise in the main from differences of a purely theological nature but rather from differing cultural experiences.

In the 1930s, however, a new situation arose. In many countries theologians proclaimed the urgent need to free theology from its captivity to cultural thought. Dialectical theologians had already launched a protest against this bondage ten years earlier, but their influence was felt in a wider international circle only about 1930 when a number of Karl Barth's works were translated. Barth and his associates advocated very strongly the basic premise of the total dependence of theology upon the revelation given in holy scripture and stressed the independence of theology from changing cultural patterns. There were also many who, although they did not follow Barth in other respects, yet agreed with him that theology should again take up its critical and prophetic task with regard to cultural life, and the life of the church itself. Reinhold Niebuhr's attack on the simplistic assumptions of the social gospel opened a new chapter in American theology. Richard Niebuhr wrote in a symposium with the significant title *The Church against the World*: "The task of the present generation appears to lie in the liberation of the church from its bondage to a corrupt civilization."[1] The witness of Russian Orthodox thinkers who had been forced into exile, particularly that of Nicolai Berdyaev, pointed in the same direction. In the field of biblical scholarship, the emphasis was now on the unity of the Bible, and on its unique character.

At that time also the nature of the church and its place in the faith became an important theme for theological reflection. New Testament scholars such as Sir Edwyn Hoskyns and C.H. Dodd in the United Kingdom and K.L. Schmidt, Martin Dibelius and H.D. Wendland in Germany showed that the church was not an invention of the period after the resurrection, but had its roots in the teaching of Jesus. A.M. Ramsey put forward a strong ecclesiology in his work *The Gospel and the Catholic Church*, while Otto Dibelius prophesied that the 20th century would be "das Jahrhundert der Kirche". Karl Barth criticized Dibelius sharply, not for emphasizing the significance of the church but for speaking of it in triumphalistic terms at a time when it was in fact weak and disobedient.

Barth himself in true Kierkegaardian fashion had at first spoken of the church as the great obstacle to the gospel. He came later to the conviction, however, that Christians had to accept responsibility for and solidarity with the church. The *Christliche Dogmatik* published in 1927 was therefore superseded by the *Kirchliche Dogmatik*, the first volume of which appeared in 1932.

Very soon after, in 1933, came the moment when the question of the independence and integrity of theology became extremely acute. The new National Socialist regime claimed that its ideology would renew the whole life of the German people and that all aspects of life should be adjusted to its norms and ideas. This gave rise to much uncertainty in the churches. Barth gave his theological and pastoral advice in the pamphlet *Theologische Existenz heute*: go on with your task, do not let yourselves be distracted from your abiding mandate to proclaim the gospel. As Hans Asmussen put it, this pamphlet had "the effect of a trumpet call". In 1934, Barth was able to render an even greater and more direct service to the church. In opposition to the "German Christians" who presented a syncretistic amalgam of Christianity and National Socialist ideology, a movement of Confessing Christians had been formed, which later became the Confessing Church. To make their position very clear, these Christians called a Confessing synod in Barmen. The document to be considered by the synod was prepared by Barth, Asmussen and Thomas Breit; it was largely Barth's work. The synod adopted the Barmen Declaration, which became the charter of the Confessing Church in the years of struggle, and which also had far-reaching ecumenical significance as a call to battle against all ideologies which sought to corrupt the church. The Barmen synod was further significant in that many theologians who had been students when the church was "the Cinderella" of theology now became the fathers and leaders of the Confessing Church. Among the younger theologians, it found a vigorous defender in Dietrich Bonhoeffer. Theologians had verily rediscovered the church.

During the church conflict in Germany, and later in similar situations in occupied countries, many theologians left their ivory towers and accepted the risk of losing their teaching posts for the sake of the church.

Another bridge between the theologians and the churches was the ecumenical movement. The conferences on Life and Work and on Faith and Order brought theologians and church leaders into closer contact. A thorough and systematic attempt to mobilize theologians to the task of clarifying the witness of the churches was undertaken by J.H. Oldham as he directed the work of preparation for the conference on Life and Work held in Oxford in 1937. He convinced the theologians that their help was really desired, was indeed indispensable. In one of the preparatory volumes he wrote: "What we have in the main is a chaos of different, and often conflicting, private opinions and not a recognized theology of the church."[2] At the Oxford conference, a valiant attempt was made to arrive at such a recognized theology with regard to the problems of society, the state and international relations. This provided at least an approach to a *magisterium*, and many church leaders and theologians found the Oxford reports a rich source of guidance during the years of the second world war. The Edinburgh conference on Faith and Order of 1937 provided another opportunity for cooperation, and at the Madras, or Tambaram, conference of the International Missionary Council in 1938, theologians from the East and the West participated in a thorough discussion of Hendrik Kraemer's challenging book *The Christian Message in a Non-Christian World*.

At the first assembly of the World Council of Churches in 1948 there were many consultants, and among them theologians were strongly represented. One delegate remarked that he saw before him in Amsterdam practically all the authors of the books in his library. When the next assembly had to be prepared, the president, Henry Van Dusen, proposed that an advisory commission of "the most creative thinkers of the churches" should be formed to prepare a document on the main theme of the assembly, "Jesus Christ, the Hope of the World", and the majority of those chosen for this task were theologians.

I was privileged to be a member of the advisory commission, whose members worked together for three years, going through many serious crises. To bring Reinhold Niebuhr and Karl Barth, or Heinrich Vogel and Henry Van Dusen to agreement on any statement was not easy, but finally a remarkable document was drawn up, one of the most substantial ever to be adopted by such a varied group. The delegates at the 1954 Evanston assembly had not experienced the same intensive ecumenical dialogue and so could accept the document only with reservations, but it had again been demonstrated how theologians, together with other "creative thinkers", could serve the church. Meanwhile, the theologians at the Montreal meeting of Faith and Order were progressing with a clarification of the problem of Tradition, and were laying the foundations for consensus on baptism, the eucharist and the ministry, which was their most important achievement.

While this progress was being made on the Protestant side, the theologians of the Roman Catholic Church found themselves in a difficult situation. After the secession of the Old Catholics, all opposition to the doctrine of papal infallibility ceased; and when the teaching authority had successfully suppressed modernist tendencies, there seemed little for Roman Catholic theologians to do but to explain the official Thomist theology and the various papal encyclicals. In the official mind, the role of the theologians was to support the *magisterium* and to provide justification for its declarations. How this conception continued to hold sway is shown by the fact that in 1956 Pius XII confirmed what Pius IX and the Vatican Council of 1870 had said on the subject.[3] A very clear formulation of the mandate of the theologians was given by Pius XII in 1954. He said: "Besides the legitimate successors of the apostles, that is to say, the Roman pontiff for the church universal and the bishops for the faithful entrusted to their care, there are in the church no other masters of divine right; but they themselves and above all the supreme Master of the Church and Vicar of Christ on earth can for their magisterial function call on collaborators and consultants and delegate the power to teach... This power remains always subordinated [to the *magisterium*] without ever becoming *sui juris*, that is to say, independent of all authority."[4] On other occasions Pius XII said that what mattered was not the *opinio theologorum* but the *sensus ecclesiae*. It would be absurd to make the theologians *magistri magisterii*.[5] Since the encyclical *Humani Generis* also made it clear that controversial matters about which the pope had pronounced his judgment should not be considered as questions open for theological study or discussion, the outlook for creative theological thinking in the Roman Catholic Church seemed dark.

In these circumstances it is all the more remarkable that new horizons opened up in the Roman Catholic Church through a "new theology" which was by no means a mere repetition of traditional teaching. It became once again clear that theology deals with a truth which cannot be repressed.

What was this "new theology"? The words have been used to describe different things. Sometimes they have been taken to mean the thought of the Jesuit theological faculty in Lyon; sometimes they refer to all new theological thinking in France, including particularly that of the Dominican centre at Le Saulchoir; sometimes the words describe all the attempts at theological renewal made by Roman Catholic theologians during that period. The raison d'être of the new movement was to overcome scholastic immobility and to arrive at a dynamic and creative theology. New theology teaches that revelation is not the communication of a system of ideas, but the manifestation of a person. This does not mean that revealed truth cannot be expressed in doctrine, but that there is always more in divine truth than can be expressed in conceptual language. The new theology is a theology of *ressourcement*, of constant returning to the chief source, the scriptures, and to the patristic tradition. It is, as was underlined most strongly in Germany, a kerygmatic theology, that is, a theology of the word of God addressed to humankind. In this view, the first task of the theologian is to reflect on the ordinary *magisterium*, which the church exercises through all its pastoral teaching, and on its distinction from the extraordinary *magisterium*, which is the definition of doctrine.

This theology can, in a profound sense, be considered as a rediscovery of the church. The writings of many of its exponents deal with the nature of the church. Congar's *Chrétiens désunis* appeared in 1937 and was followed by a great number of ecclesiological studies which make him the church father of the 20th century in that field. In 1938, Henri de Lubac published *Catholicisme*, which was followed by *Corpus Mysticum* and *Méditation sur l'Eglise*. Hugo Rahner wrote on *Mater Ecclesia* and Robert Grosche on *Pilgernde Kirche*, both seeking to uncover the original meaning of the church which had become distorted by institutionalism and juridical concepts. They found that there were dimensions of the church in the Bible and in tradition which had to be brought again to light, and stood for the wholeness of the church as the people of God over against the church as the hierarchy.

Inevitably, this new dynamic conception of theology met with suspicion in the Vatican, with its static and scholastic view of the subject. In 1946, a Dominican, Réginald Garrigou Lagrange, launched an attack on the theologians in Lyon, contending that what they were teaching was really modernism. The accusation was false, for their concern was not to make the church "intellectually inhabitable", as the modernists had tried to do, but to liberate its inherent creative power. The encyclical *Humani Generis* of 1950 showed further how greatly the Vatican was alarmed by the new movement. It spoke of people who love "new things", and who pass easily from contempt for scholastic teaching to a lack of respect, even contempt, for the *magisterium* of the church. The role of theologians is, it stated further, "to show in which way the truths taught by the living *magisterium* are to be found explicitly or implicitly in the scriptures and in tradition". In those years, a considerable number of theologians were dismissed from their posts, or found it very difficult to have their writings accepted. It is said that Karl Rahner's work went through the hands of seven censors before it could be published.

NOTES

[1] Richard Niebuhr, *The Church against the World*, Chicago, Willett, Clark, 1935, p.124.
[2] J.H. Oldham, *The Church and Its Function in Society*, London, Allen & Unwin, 1937, p.163.
[3] Congar, *Les théologiens et l'Eglise*, p.115.
[4] *Ibid.*
[5] *Ibid.*

11. The *Magistri* Participate in the *Magisterium*

The Second Vatican Council was of very great significance in a number of ways. One which has perhaps not been sufficiently underlined, but has had a profound influence on the life of the church, is the fact that there occurred a meeting of minds between bishops and theologians which was unprecedented in scale and intensity.

We have seen that the only theologians who played an important role at the First Vatican Council were the Roman school, defenders of neo-scholasticism. At the Second Vatican Council, the situation was very different. In December 1962 Congar recorded his impressions from Rome: "It should be understood that, in addition to the meetings of bishops in national or regional groups, there is a council of theologians. More than a hundred, perhaps two hundred theologians have accompanied the bishops, many of them men who are playing an active, often creative and dynamic, role in the life of worldwide Catholicism, especially in the European region." In 1980, looking back on the council, he said: "An exemplary collaboration [*collaboration modèle*] was achieved there between the fathers and the 'experts'."[1]

In fact, many bishops were at least as eager as university students and seminarists to learn about the newer trends in theology. Some of the theologians received more invitations to give lectures than they could accept. There was substance in the remark of a bishop who said, half-seriously, that one began to wonder who represented the *magisterium*. In facilitating the meeting of bishops, who for the most part had studied prior to the rise of the new theology and of theologians who only a few years previously had been regarded as having dangerous thoughts, Pope John was taking a considerable risk, for it was clearly impossible to avoid conflict between the protagonists of *semper eadem* and those of *semper reformanda*. It was, however, a risk which the pope was prepared to take for the sake of the church. At the end of the first session he said that there had been understandable but nevertheless worrying differences of opinion, but this showed that the children of God have a holy freedom in the church. Theologians were able to make their full contribution in drafting and rewriting the documents to be put to the vote. Thus, when a very delicate situation arose in the preparation of the schema on revelation, the commission formed to prepare a new draft was composed of seven bishops and twenty-one theologians, including Rahner and Congar.

The studies published on the elaboration of most of the council documents show that it was largely due to the quality of the theologians' work that the Second Vatican Council produced declarations and constitutions of substance, directives for the church in the years to come.

It would have been appropriate on that occasion to give a clearer definition of the role of theologians in the church or, at least, to express recognition of their indispensable task, but this was not done. It is true that, in the Constitution on Divine Revelation, there are words of praise for biblical scholars, for their study of the Bible as the soul of theology, and their constant rejuvenation of theology by the word of God.[2] Nothing was said, however, about the prophetic and critical role of theology in the life of the church. When the teaching function of the church was mentioned, it was underlined that "through the Holy Spirit given to them, bishops have been made true and authentic teachers of the faith, pontiffs and shepherds".[3] Further, there is in the Constitution on Divine Revelation the somewhat cryptic sentence that the task of the authentic interpretation of the word of God, whether written or handed on, has been entrusted exclusively to the living, teaching office of the church.[4] Was this not a warning to theologians not to think of themselves as having a share in the *magisterium*? Although the council had much to say about the hierarchy, priests, religious orders, school-teachers and the laity, its statements shed no light on the place of theologians in the church, nor is there any mention of the very fruitful collaboration between bishops and theologians which had made the council memorable. It may have been due to concentration on the problem of collegiality between the pope and the bishops that the no less important collegiality between the *magistri* and the bearers of the official *magisterium* was not openly discussed, so that all the theologians could learn about their relation to bishops was that they should show loyal obedience to the episcopal authority.[5]

As far as the nature of the *magisterium* was concerned, the council did not modify the declarations of 1870. Some phrases in the explanatory note added to the Constitution on the Church seemed, by the pope's decision, even to add weight to the *ex sese* of 1870. The note stated that the pope "proceeds according to his own discretion" and "can always exercise his authority as he chooses". On the other hand, it was stated in the Constitution on Divine Revelation that "the teaching office is not above the word of God, but serves it".[6] The significance of this very important statement is, however, weakened by other statements in which scripture, Tradition and the teaching office seem to be placed on the same level. Karl Barth, who praised the Constitution on Divine Revelation for its concentration on the Bible, saw in this linking of scripture, Tradition and *magisterium* "an attack of weakness" (*Schwächeanfall*) suffered by the council.[7]

When the council was over the theologians were deeply grateful for, from their point of view, they had reaped a greater harvest than they had dared to expect. With regard to ecclesiology, *ressourcement*, ecumenism, religious liberty and the task of the church in society, the council had accepted the position for which the new theologians had pleaded. Moreover, the way in which their collaboration had been welcomed at the council seemed to indicate that they would in future enjoy full freedom to perform their creative and critical task. One of the most penetrating books on the new situation was *Aggiornamento* published in 1968 by Father T.M. Schoof, Prof. Schillebeeckx's assistant. Its sub-title is *The Break-Through of a New Catholic Theology*, and its conclusion is that Catholic theologians had now to become accustomed to the position which they had regained. Karl Barth, a severe critic of the Roman Catholic Church, was so deeply impressed by the council that he wished to enter into personal contact with Roman Catholic church leaders and theologians. To this end, he made a journey in 1966 and reported on it in *Ad Limina Apostolorum*, stating that he had come to know a church and a theology which were on the move – a movement which was slow, but nevertheless real and irreversible, which was something he wished he could say of his own confession.[8]

Kristen Skydsgaard of Denmark came to a similar conclusion, and said that the Lutherans had now to revise their conception of the Roman Catholic Church: "For who among us had expected that this church which was famous and notorious for its immobility, was capable of so much change? Naturally she has remained the same [church] as we shall see in the future, but still, she has become another church. To understand this paradox is to understand the council."[9]

NOTES

[1] Congar, *Les théologiens et l'Eglise*, pp.12,128.
[2] Second Vatican Council, *Constitution on Divine Revelation*, 23-24.
[3] Second Vatican Council, *Decree on the Bishops*, 2.
[4] Second Vatican Council, *Constitution on Divine Revelation*, 10.
[5] Second Vatican Council, *Decree on Priestly Formation*, 4.
[6] Second Vatican Council, *Constitution on Divine Revelation*, 10.
[7] Karl Barth, *Ad Limina Apostolorum*, Zurich, EVZ-Verlag, 1967, pp.52,29.
[8] *Ibid.*, p.17.
[9] Kristen Skydsgaard, *Wir sind gefragt*, p.195.

12. Once More the Parting of the Ways?

After the council, most Roman Catholic theologians felt that a new day had dawned for their profession and calling. A three-volume symposium was published in 1967 in which many prominent theologians presented their impressions of the council. It is entitled *Die Autorität der Freiheit* (Authority of Freedom). The general introduction by the editor, Johann Christoph Hampe, bears the title "Libertas Christiana"; and Gottfried Müller's contribution on "Catholic Theology after the Council" stated: "This is the new situation of theology. The council has given theology back its freedom [wieder freigegeben]." In 1969, a declaration signed by 1360 theologians in fifty-three countries was published under the title "The Freedom of Theologians and of Theology". It began by stating that this freedom in the service of the church had been restored by the Second Vatican Council.

Theologians therefore believed that the council was not an end but a beginning or, as Karl Rahner put it, the beginning of a beginning. In their view, the documents of the council were signposts to show the direction in which theology should advance. Before long, however, it became clear that this was not the only possible conception of the significance of the council. Many responsible leaders of the church thought that the council's decisions were to be regarded not as signposts, but rather as boundary stones. In their view, the council had introduced so many new elements and ideas into the life of the church that time must be given for the church to digest them. For these churchmen, the council meant: "So far, but not further for a long time to come."

Thus, one year later, Alfredo Cardinal Ottaviani of the Sacred Congregation for the Doctrine of the Faith wrote to all bishops a letter asking whether ten specifically mentioned heresies were propagated in their dioceses. In their declaration of 1969, in addition to expressing their joy at the freedom granted to them, the 1360 theologians had expressed their profound concern that it should not again be endangered. They had affirmed the teaching authority of the pope and the bishops, but stated that this pastoral office should not push aside nor be a hindrance to the scientific teaching task of the theologians.

In the nervous climate of the revolutionary year 1968 the encyclical *Humanae Vitae* appeared, and revealed a deep polarization in the life of the church. The agitation was not so much due to the subject matter, although the main point of the encyclical, the refusal to allow artificial means of contraception, was a matter of vital interest and concern to the immense majority of Roman Catholics. Whatever form the Vatican's decision on that matter might have taken, it would have caused discussion. This does not, however, explain the depth and comprehensive character of the ensuing public reaction. What caused the greatest shock was the fact that the encyclical seemed to show that the Second Vatican Council had made no difference as far as the functioning of the *magisterium* was concerned. *Humanae Vitae* appeared to have all the defects of the pre-conciliar period, as the decision taken by the pope was clearly not an example of the collegiality which the council had advocated. He had not accepted the advice of the majority of the advisory committee set up to study the problem, nor had there been adequate consultation with the theologians, most of whom were in favour of greater freedom. The concern expressed by the council about problems of poverty and hunger in countries with a rapidly increasing population had not been adequately considered.

The real reason why the pope had been unwilling to adopt a more liberal policy was that he did not wish to act in contradiction to the position of his predecessors, particularly that of Pius XI who, in 1930, had issued the encyclical *Casti Connubii* in opposition to the tolerant attitude on contraception shown by the Anglican bishops at the Lambeth conference of the same year. This was a sign of precisely that obsession with the past, with continuity and irreformability, which John XXIII had sought to overcome with his call to a genuine *aggiornamento* (bringing up to date).

At the same time, the encyclical stressed the issue of authority, for its emphasis was: "This is true because the pope says it is true." It was inevitable therefore that there should be widespread discussion on its doctrinal significance.

The answers given to questioners by official or semi-official authorities showed that there was no clear consensus among them. The official commentator, Monsignor Lumbruschini, stated at a press conference at the Vatican that the encyclical was an authentic but not an infallible document, but Cardinal Felici, who had been the general secretary of the Second Vatican Council, wrote soon afterwards that the fact that the encyclical had not been promulgated *ex cathedra* did not mean that it was not infallible, for truth can be certain and should be accepted with obedience if it represents the traditional and continuous teaching of the *magisterium*, as was the case in *Humanae Vitae*. On the other hand, some regional bishops' conferences went a long way in a more liberal direction. In August 1968, the Belgian bishops declared that the encyclical was not to be considered as infallible and irrevocable and that the faithful were not obliged to accept it unconditionally and absolutely, as is required in the case of a dogmatic definition.

The result of this was that the whole problem of the nature of the *magisterium* and, in particular, the meaning of the term "infallibility" again became acute. In 1970, Hans Küng published a book under the title *Unfehlbar?* – in English, *Infallible?* He showed that the formula used at the First and Second Vatican Councils to describe infallibility had not provided a clear and coherent conception of the *magisterium* and asked whether it was not time to revise it. He suggested that indefectibility, the guidance of the church by the Holy Spirit, is a more adequate concept, in spite of its shortcomings. With regard to the question of teaching authority, Küng considers as a limitation the theory that church leaders are the sole authority in matters of doctrine. It is his belief that to make of these leaders the only teachers results in the bishops monopolizing the *charismata* in the "hierocracy" of the shepherds, which was in contradiction to the New Testament message.[1] The right authentically to proclaim and explain the Christian message is, he states, not reserved to any one group. Moreover, theologians are not merely delegates of the *magisterium*, but have their own specific calling.[2] Küng does not deny that the *magisterium* should intervene in situations in which the church is threatened by widespread heresy, but he believes that this should be the exception and not the rule.[3]

Küng's book led to a debate in which old alliances were broken and new ones formed. It became clear that he was not one lonely dissenter but that other prominent theologians shared a number of his convictions. In 1971, however, the Sacred Congregation for the Doctrine of the Faith decided to investigate the main theses contained in *Unfehlbar?* It is significant that the very first question asked by the congregation concerned the passage in which Küng maintained that the authentic proclamation and explanation of the Christian message are not reserved to any one group; the congregation called attention to passages in the documents of the Second Vatican Council which state that the authentic interpretation of the word of God has been entrusted exclusively to the *magisterium* of the church.[4] Küng did not withdraw his statement, so his *missio canonica*, or right to teach, was rescinded in 1979.

The reaction among theologians to this Roman intervention was extremely strong. They had believed that such disciplinary measures taken without adequate discussion with the theologian concerned belonged to the pre-conciliar past, and now speculated whether the days of Pius XII might not be returning.

The problem of the nature of the *magisterium* and of relations between bishops and theologians had by this time become the subject of study and controversy in many parts of the church. In the American journal *Theology Today* of October 1979, the Roman Catholic theologian Bernard J. Cooke wrote: "The recent disputes about authority within the Catholic church have centred about teaching authority and (somewhat derivatively) sacramental authority. What is at question is the notion of *magisterium*, whether or not a given group in the church, more specifically the episcopacy as centred in the papacy, can lay claim by virtue of its *official* position to a fullness of teaching authority so great that it can pass judgment upon any other exercise of teaching in the church." At the end of 1977, the United States Bishops' Committee on Doctrine began a series of meetings where bishops and theologians held an ongoing discussion about the *magisterium*. A first report published in 1980 stated, "There was unanimous agreement that the separation of bishops and theologians is a serious problem facing the church today."[5] The most striking of the papers prepared for the committee was written by the well-known theologian Avery Dulles, and was summarized in the report. It stated that the "structures commonly regarded as Catholic today are relatively new and thus do not reflect God's unalterable design for his church". Dulles asked "whether we can credibly view the bishop as the 'chief teacher' in our time", and also "whether theologians individually, or at least corporately, could be acknowledged as possessing true doctrinal and magisterial authority", an idea which he recalled was well founded in tradition. In the post-Tridentine period, the many sources of teaching authority recognized in the New Testament and in earlier church history had been reduced to one, the hierarchical, which was itself progressively reduced to the single voice of the papacy. In the third chapter on the "Constitution on the Church" of the Second Vatican Council, the new doctrine of collegiality was set beside that of the monarchical papalism of Vatican I without any genuine reconciliation of the two points of view. Vatican II, through its skilful resuscitation of the patristic model of representation and consensus, did supply a helpful corrective to the juridicism and papalism of the post-Tridentine and neo-scholastic periods. It did not, however, provide a new or consistent paradigm of the *magisterium* and thus left the task of completing its programme to the post-conciliar church.

The complexity of the problem and the pluralism of views in Roman Catholic theology are further illustrated by the fact that a position differing from all those just described was taken by Yves Congar, who had studied the question of ecclesiology more thoroughly than had anyone else in our time. While he was convinced that the doctrine formulated by the First Vatican Council "will have to be the object of a re-reception which might just as well be called a reinterpretation",[6] he felt that Küng and those who shared his ideas were not taking sufficiently seriously the traditional teaching that bishops are pastors and doctors. In Congar's view, the combination in bishops of these two functions was an important characteristic of ecclesiology.[7]

The creation of the International Commission of Theologians as a permanent body where theologians can express their views on the main issues of church life has apparently not led to a true dialogue between them and the official leaders of the church. Congar is of the opinion that the proposals put forward by the commission have had no influence on the life of the church, and that the Roman authorities have used it only insofar as it strengthens their own position. It is further of significance that the bishops' synod meets without theological consultants.

Recently, the Sacred Congregation for the Doctrine of the Faith started an investigation of the theological teaching of Edward Schillebeeckx. Documents relating to this investigation, published in 1980, illustrate very clearly that the Roman authorities have very little sympathy for the new paths of theology. In a "conversation", which in fact took the form of an examination, the representatives of the Sacred Congregation and Schillebeeckx were at cross-purposes. His books emerge from a pastoral and apologetic concern to show that faith in Christ has a real foundation in history and to tell the story of Jesus in such a way that modern man, inside and outside the church, can understand it. His examiner, however, wanted to hear only traditional answers in traditional language.

An American theologian recently claimed to have identified a new phenomenon in the Roman Catholic Church in his country – a "loyal opposition". The same might be said of many countries, with theologians forming the "loyal opposition". Karl Rahner, in a hard-hitting article entitled "I Protest",[8] criticized the then archbishop of Munich, Joseph Ratzinger, for refusing to approve the appointment of Prof. J.B. Metz to the university in that city. He pointed out that all too often the authorities, knowing that they need not fear a revolt, take unfair advantage of the loyalty of faithful members to their church. Church members could at least, however, raise their voices in protest.

In these ways, theologians in the Roman Catholic Church are increasingly fulfilling the critical function of theology. It is precisely because they want to be loyal to the great tradition of the church that they ask their questions and react against any move to obscure that great tradition.

On the national level, attempts are being made to build bridges between the hierarchy and the theologians. In 1980 in the United States, bishops and theologians participating in discussions organized by the

Bishops' Commission on Doctrine resolved: "In overcoming difficulties, the basic relationship has to be one of collaboration. Bishops and theologians need to meet, get to know one another and express a common concern for seeking solutions to common problems." When the assistant bishop of Paris, Monsignor Daniel Pézeril, visited the theological faculties in France as a representative of the doctrinal bureau of the French Roman Catholic Church, he would urge theologians "non pas d'exister moins mais d'exister plus et mieux", begging them to ensure that the self-regulation exercised by theologians be effective.[9] In 1968 Dutch bishops, in reply to an enquiry by Cardinal Ottaviani, already referred to this process of self-correction in theological studies. They said: "If the *magisterium* would have more confidence in the theologians, possible exaggerations would disappear, and that more quickly through free discussion than by lists of errors."[10] Further, when Edward Schillebeeckx's orthodoxy was questioned by Rome, Johannes Cardinal Willebrands made a public statement to the effect that he was convinced of the correct ecclesial attitude, and of the faith, of Schillebeeckx.

In this period there was also a parting of the ways between theologians and church leaders in the Reformation churches, but it had different characteristics. There had long been, in most of these churches, a variety of theological tendencies. Now, however, this diversification became even more accentuated and led to a great deal of confusion. The time seemed past in which outstanding theologians like Barth and Niebuhr had, through their international influence, been able to create at least partial coherence. John Bennett, a former president of Union Theological Seminary in New York, said in 1979: "There is some ferment but less theological leadership than at any other period of my life-time."[11] Biblical theology which, with its emphasis on the unity of the Bible, had been dominant in many churches and the backbone of the ecumenical movement was now criticized for being a systematic construction rather than a true interpretation of biblical data. The main interest of theologians was now to show the diversity of theologies in the New Testament, through which they explained the diversity of theology in the history of the church. Further, there is today a proliferation of specialized theologies. These are described by terms such as "feminist" or "black"; they announce a special goal such as liberation or ecology, or reveal a particular regional cultural approach, such as third-world theology.

There is no doubt that all these concerns must be theologically interpreted and given their rightful place in the thinking of the church, but it is strange that no one seems to be working on a theology for the church itself – not the church as a self-centred institution, but as the *una sancta* proclaiming the one great central message of the gospel to all nations.

In the theology of the 1960s and 1970s, the previous generation's rediscovery of the meaning of the church seemed to have lost its force. This was due partly to the widespread anti-institutionalism of the period, by which the church was regarded as part of the hated Establishment. There was also a sense of frustration resulting from the failure of the churches to respond adequately to the tremendous challenges presented by the chaotic world of the period. To be sure, there were some signs of renewal, but in general the churches did not seem to have realized that a total revision of their relationship to the surrounding society was required.

Not a few theologians expressed the conviction that the theology of the previous generation had been too "church-centred", and proposed a "theology of the apostolate" in which the church was seen simply as an instrument of the God-given mission. The Dutch theologian J.C. Hoekendijk said that there was nothing which the church could claim for its own, not even ecclesiology. He believed that the ecumenical movement should be concerned, not with the unity and fellowship of the churches, but rather with their common corporate witness to the kingdom of God.[12] Others elaborated a conception of the church as an instrument in the context of a "horizontal theology". It was felt that the church ought to be dealing with the business of the world, rather than with its own business. What was required of it was "worldmanship" rather than "churchmanship". The church should be "a church for others"; it had no significance apart from its task of bringing justice and peace to the world.

In this situation, it is not surprising that the nature of the *magisterium* or teaching authority of the church has to be reconsidered. It is clearer than ever before that the church's duty is to justify the faith which is its raison d'être. Church conflicts in totalitarian situations and the challenge of an aggressive neo-paganism are forcing all churches to reconsider the context of their witness. A church which refuses to be a confessing church no longer has any credibility.

But by what criteria is the loyalty of a church to its mission of witness and confession to be judged? It was judged in the past by its conformity with traditional creeds and confessions, but many theologians have now become convinced this is inadequate. Doctrinal statements are made in terms which are of necessity conditioned by their historical context. They can therefore never be taken as definitive, but need constant reinterpretation. Moreover, preservation of the faith requires far more than simply the preservation of doctrinal purity. Orthopraxis or proper action is as important as orthodoxy in the life of the church. A sentence in my address to the Uppsala assembly of the World Council of Churches in 1968 was received, greatly to my surprise, with a very strong positive reaction. I said: "It must become clear that church members who deny in fact their responsibility for the needy in any part of the world are just as much guilty of heresy as those who deny this or that article of the faith." Today's tendency to make orthopraxis the chief or only criterion can also lead to a form of heresy. But it is gain and not loss when what the church does, and how it lives, is judged as seriously as what it says.

As to the way in which the *magisterium* should be exercised, there is much uncertainty. Many feel that the old methods of control are survivals from the time of Constantine – which might be better described as the time of Theodosius, because it was during the reign of Emperor Theodosius I (A.D. 379-395) that heresy became a crime which could be punished by law. In our present situation, and with our present understanding of the nature of the church, any supervision must have a purely pastoral character. Further, this supervision cannot be in the hands of any one particular group or order in the church, for the church as a whole is responsible to its Lord, and every church member has the right of appeal to the judgment of the whole church. This very important right is particularly a right of the theologians. Even if mistaken opinions have some temporary success, theologians, left in freedom to perform their specific mission, will usually correct exaggerations or heresies arising among them. Such theological derailments as the proposal to eliminate the Old Testament from holy scripture, or the "God-is-dead" theology, have practically disappeared as a result of self-regulation exercised by theologians. There was no need of intervention by any other authority.

It will, however, be clearly seen that those responsible for leadership in the churches are in a difficult situation. On the one hand there is a crying need to give guidance to church members in this time of great religious confusion while, on the other hand, expressing firm belief on almost any controversial theological issue can prove so difficult as sometimes to appear impossible.

NOTES

[1] Hans Küng, *Unfehlbar?*, Zurich, Benziger, 1970, p.188.
[2] *Ibid.,* pp.191-92.
[3] *Ibid.,* p.195.
[4] Constitution on Divine Revelation, 10.
[5] "Origins", 7 Feb. 1980.
[6] Congar, *Voices of Unity*, p.28.
[7] Congar, *Les théologiens et l'Eglise.*
[8] *Public Forum*, 16 Nov. 1979.
[9] Congar, *Les théologiens et l'Eglise*, p.62.
[10] T.M. Schoof, *Aggiornamento*, Baarn, Het. Wereldvenster, 1968, p.279.
[11] John Bennett, *Christianity and Crisis*, 15 Jan. 1979.
[12] J.C. Hoekendijk, *De Kerk Binnenste Buiten*, Amsterdam, Ten Have, 1964, pp.51,53.

13. Authority and Freedom
in Eastern Orthodoxy

Can the Eastern Orthodox churches make a positive contribution to the solution of the problem of relations between the *magistri* and the *magisterium?* At the beginning of this century, Western theologians and other churchmen would have given a negative answer to this question. In his best-seller *What Is Christianity*, published in 1900, the renowned church historian Adolf von Harnack declared that Eastern Orthodoxy was an anachronism. Further, in 1913 he wrote that the Eastern churches represented the Christianity of the 3rd century in petrified form.[1] This judgment showed that he knew a great deal about the past and very little about the present conditions of Eastern Orthodoxy. In those thirteen years, especially in Russia, a great interest had developed in the question of the significance of Orthodoxy in culture. Philosophers, writers and clergymen, strongly stimulated by the works of Dostoevsky and Soloviev, met regularly to discuss religious problems. In 1907, Nicolai Berdyaev published a book with the significant title *The New Religious Consciousness.* Soon after, when atheistic ideology attacked the church, it became even clearer that Christianity in Russia was not a fossil. "A church which produces many thousands of martyrs cannot be as frozen or dead as has been its reputation."[2] In 1920, the Ecumenical Patriarchate of Constantinople took the unprecedented step of proposing to all other churches the formation of a worldwide "league of churches".

It seems to me that there are three reasons why the Orthodox churches have been misunderstood. First, there was simply a lack of contact, or at least of the right kind of contact. Bitter memories remained both of the conflict in which the Teutonic knights attacked the prince of Novgorod, who became St Alexander Nevski, and of the fourth crusade, in which Latin Christians had snatched the city of Constantinople from the Orthodox. The bitterness was increased by campaigns of proselytism conducted by both Roman Catholics and Protestants. Even the efforts to arrive at reunion seemed to have done more harm than good. The council of Florence held in the 15th century to achieve reunion produced a strong anti-Roman reaction in the East, and the rapprochement in the 17th century of the patriarch of Constantinople, Cyrillus Lucaris, and the Protestant church was greeted by the Orthodox with great suspicion of Protestantism.

The second reason why Eastern Orthodoxy has been misunderstood in the West is that it has rarely had freedom to express its true spirit. During long periods of its history, it has been oppressed by non-Christian or anti-Christian regimes. Even when the government was Christian, the official policy of "symphony" between the church and the state was applied in a way which gave the government the main role and the church only a secondary one. The famous Pobedonostsev, who was practically a dictator in the Russian Orthodox Church in the last years of the czarist regime, perfected this authoritarian system to such a degree that the church became one of the main pillars of the absolute monarchy.

There is a third reason for the misunderstanding of which we are speaking. It is the reluctance of the Orthodox church to define itself. Georges Florovsky wrote: "The very nature of the church can be depicted and described rather than properly defined."[3] Sergei Bulgakov declared: "Come and see! One can come to know the church only through experience, by grace and participation in its life."[4] Congar believes that the genius of Orthodoxy is not only that it does not feel the need to define, but that it feels the need not to define.[5] For Eastern Christians "Orthodoxy" is primarily understood in terms of doxology, the true worship, rather than as a rigid system of doctrinal formulations. Moreover, there is only a limited number of dogmatic formulas which have definitive authority for dogma can be defined only by an ecumenical council recognized and received by the whole church, and no such council has been held since the 8th century.

In such a context it is clear that the relations between theologians and the teaching authority in the Eastern church are bound to be different from those in Western churches. The Eastern Orthodox theologian has considerable freedom in his theological thinking. Paul Evdokimov considers the principle *in dubiis libertas*, which implies a minimum of dogma and no limitation on theological opinion, to be the golden rule of Orthodoxy.[6] All theological statements which have not been accepted by the whole church are *theologoumena*. Chrestos Androutsos in his *Dogmatics of the Eastern Church*[7] remarks that the Orthodox theologian plays a specially important role. A Roman Catholic theologian has to take into account the fixed dogmatic formulas of the council of Trent and the Vatican Council, as well as papal definitions, but the Orthodox theologian has freedom to formulate and classify the *theologoumena*. When the Patriarchate of Moscow in 1935 declared that Bulgakov's sophiological theology was incompatible with Orthodox doctrine, the theologian replied that such a condemnation was not in keeping with the genius of the Eastern Orthodox church.

Orthodoxy has always recognized the existence of different schools of theology and different opinions, and believes that, without freedom of theological thinking within the limits of the dogma of the church, there can be no living theology.[8] But this "apparent disorder of Orthodoxy which goes so far that it gives the impression of anarchy", as Evdokimov writes,[9] is not a form of individualism but its contrary. "The practical result of the 'nebulosity' with which tradition is defined in Orthodoxy is the deep sense that the entire church – and not only the 'authorities' whatever they may be – patriarchs or councils – is responsible for tradition."[10] This conviction was expressed in the often quoted statement of the Eastern patriarchs made in response to an encyclical of Pope Pius IX, where they stated: "Among us, novelties cannot be introduced by patriarchs or councils, for the guardian of religion is the whole body of the church, that is, the people who desire to conserve its faith unchanged." This is borne out by the following formulation given by Johannes Karmires: "The consciousness of the clergy and the laity as a whole, of clergymen and laymen, of those who command and those who obey, of masters and servants, of men and women who are members of the body of Christ and form together the *pleroma*, the totality, the body of the church, which in Orthodoxy is considered as the only infallible authority."[11] In Russian theology, this conception of the nature of the church is known as *sobornost*. It has been worked out most fully by the prophetic layman, Aleksei Chomiakov, who considered it to be the doctrine which most specifically distinguishes Orthodoxy from both Roman Catholicism and Protestantism. Although Chomiakov's ideas have been criticized, they have exerted a deep influence on Russian theology. Stefan Zankov summarizes *sobornost* ecclesiology as follows: "An inner all-embracing unity, a symphony in faith and in life, inward and outward, a harmonious unity of a multitude, in which the church is neither the church according to each individual nor the church according to the bishop of Rome, but the church as a whole, catholic, according to the faith of all believers in their unity."[12]

Chomiakov claimed that *sobornost* can be found only in Eastern Orthodoxy and condemned Roman Catholicism and Protestantism for having abandoned this conception of the church. Berdyaev, however, although he had a great admiration for Chomiakov, considered this sharply polemical attitude towards the other confessions as a serious error.[13] The truth which *sobornost* ecclesiology seeks to express has found advocates in all churches, for it is the truth inherent in the *koinonia* of the New Testament, the communion in which there is no external nor imposed authority, no monopoly of power, but a constant living, sharing, witnessing together, as St Paul describes in the image of the body with its various members.

Orthodox theologians have rendered a great service to the other churches by denying that each church must choose either authority or freedom. Quoting the second epistle to the Corinthians, chapter 3, verse 17, "Where the spirit of the Lord is, there is freedom", Bulgakov says that the *sobornost* principle has a corrective function.[14] It can correct an authoritarian type of *magisterium* concentrated on maintaining its institutional cohesion, and it can also correct that egocentricism which, in our modern age, threatens to cause the disintegration of all churches, and which has rightly been described as "do-it-yourself religion". There is a crying need for theologians who perform their task in full freedom, but with a deep consciousness of being rooted in, and nourished by, the *una sancta*.

NOTES

[1] Adolf von Harnack, "The Spirit of the Church in the East", *Proceedings of the Academy of Science*, Berlin, 1913.

[2] Edmund Schlink, *Der kommende Christus und die kirchlichen Traditionen*, Göttingen, Vandenhoeck & Ruprecht, 1961, p.221.

[3] Georges Florovsky, *The Universal Church in God's Design*, London, SCM Press, 1948, p.44.

[4] Sergei Bulgakov, *L'Orthodoxie*, Paris, Librairie Félix Alcan, 1932, p.4.

[5] Yves Congar, *Diversités et communion*, Paris, Cerf, 1982, p.93.

[6] Paul Evdokimov, *L'Orthodoxie*, Neuchâtel, Delachaux et Niestlé, 1959, p.194.

[7] Quoted in Congar, *Diversités et communion*, p.77.

[8] Sergei Bulgakov, *Orient und Occident*, March 1936, pp.12,28.

[9] Evdokimov, *L'Orthodoxie*, p.41.

[10] John Meyendorff, *St. Vladimir's Theological Quarterly*, 1982, p.3.

[11] Quoted in Schlink, *Der kommende Christus und die kirchlichen Traditionen*, p.192.

[12] Stefan Zankov, *Die Orthodoxe Kirche des Ostens in ökumenischer Sicht*, Zurich, Zwingli-Verlag, 1946, p.92.

[13] Reinhard Slenczka, *Ostkirche und Ökumene*, Göttingen, Vandenhoeck & Ruprecht, 1962, p.74.

[14] Sergei Bulgakov, *Congrès de théologie,* Athènes, 1936, p.130.

14. *Magistri* and *Magisterium* in the Ecumenical Dialogue

The ecumenical dialogue has shown that the most difficult problems to be solved on the way to unity are those of ecclesiology, and the most difficult issues in ecclesiology are the questions: What is the nature of the *magisterium?* To whom has been given the mandate and authority to be the agent or agents of the *magisterium?*

Pope Paul VI raised this problem in the encyclical *Ecclesiam Suam* of 1964. He said that he was saddened by the thought that while he sought the reconciliation of the separated churches, he was himself considered, because of the primacy of the papacy, to be an obstacle to that reconciliation. He claimed, however, that without the pope the Catholic church would no longer be itself, and without the supreme and decisive pastoral office of Peter in the church, unity would be lost.

The real problem is not whether a pastoral office of a Petrine character is desirable or necessary. The real problem is the papacy as it exists today. With full respect for the pope's appeal, it must be said that discussions of the papacy will inevitably be controversial. Franz Leenhardt calls it "the hard core of the problem of unity", and goes on to quote G. Desaifve, who, from the Roman Catholic standpoint, calls it "the number one problem of ecumenism".[1] Yves Congar has written: "Unity appears to be impossible with a papacy such as history has made it."[2] Indeed the most crucial development in that history was the elaboration of the papal understanding of the papal office in doctrinal and juridical formulas which the Roman Catholic Church considers to be of permanent validity.

The definitions of the First Vatican Council, as completed by the Second, and particularly those in the "Nota Praevia Explicativa" attached to the document *Lumen Gentium*, describe the universal jurisdiction of the pope and his supreme *magisterium* as allowing him always to exercise his authority as he chooses, "as is demanded by the office itself". It is true that the Second Vatican Council also emphasized the collegiality of the pope and the bishops, but the pope was still seen to be the one and only arbiter. I cannot see that any other church can accept this conception of the *magisterium,* for to do so would be to surrender an essential element of ecclesiological doctrine which it has proclaimed to its members throughout its history.

It would certainly be possible to elaborate a conception of the papacy and its magisterial office which many different churches could accept, and this has been done in a number of ecumenical conferences and in bilateral conversations. These proposed conceptions have in common the idea that the decision taken in 1870 about the universal jurisdiction of the pope should be "re-received" or "reinterpreted", so that it would become acceptable to other churches. This would imply that the dogmatic definition of the universal jurisdiction of the pope would not be applied to the churches entering into unity with the Roman Catholic Church. It is, however, not easy to imagine how a *magisterium* would operate which believes itself to be of universal validity in principle, but does not insist on acceptance of that universality by churches to which it is united. There is in any case no indication that the authorities of the Roman Catholic Church are willing to consider such a far-reaching revision of its position. In fact, the "Observations" that the Sacred Congregation for the Doctrine of the Faith made on the report of the Anglican-Roman Catholic International Commission and published in 1982 point in the opposite direction. Although the commission went a long way towards accepting the primacy of the pope, it was the opinion of the congregation that no substantial agreement had been reached, because the commission had not adopted fully and without qualification the definitions of the First and Second Vatican Councils. It is not surprising that the churches engaged in conversation with Rome have asked whether there is any meaning to a dialogue in which one of the partners simply demands submission to its own position.

We must not forget, however, that there is another side to this problem. This is the fact that the absence of, or inadequate function of, the *magisterium* is a serious handicap in the seeking of church unity. Speaking of the bilateral conversations between the Roman Catholic Church and other churches, Johannes Cardinal Willebrands has asked whether, in the many churches and ecclesial communities without a hierarchical structure such as that of Rome, there is any official authority which can take a final decision binding in conscience on the faith and life of their members.[3] In the Malta report of 1971 on the conversations between the Roman Catholic Church and the Lutheran World Federation, it is stated that a particular difficulty had been the fact that the Lutherans have no authoritative statement of their faith later than the confessions of the 16th century; other churches are faced with the same problem. The confessional alliances or families of churches involved in the bilateral conversations do not have the ecclesial status required to speak with the authority of a *magisterium*. Church bodies in dialogue with the Roman Catholic Church and with one another must therefore decide how to develop a conception of the *magisterium* that would enable them to state clearly what they believe today yet not abandon their traditional position on the responsibility of the church as a whole for the faith of its members, and on the freedom to be accorded to theologians.

It also seems to me desirable, even inevitable, that the role of theologians in the church, in particular the question of their freedom, should be discussed by the churches. Yves Congar has noted that the measures recently taken against theologians in the Roman Catholic Church have contributed to a revival among Protestants of latent anxieties and hesitations concerning relations with Rome.[4]

When Hans Küng's *missio canonica* was withdrawn, many Protestant theologians expressed deep concern at this interference with theological freedom and the way in which it was done. They were right, in my opinion, because they felt that in two ways "this concerns us" [*nostra res agitur*]. It concerned them firstly because the issues treated by Küng and condemned in Rome were high on the ecumenical agenda. Secondly, they could not help but ask themselves what would happen to them if their church should be united to that of Rome. Peder Højen has gone as far as to suggest that, in the light of Rome's decision, the Reformation churches would give up all dreams of a possible reform of the papacy; the same line has been taken by Jürgen Moltmann.[5] It is therefore urgently necessary to discuss the matter in bilateral meetings.

What we have said so far about the ecumenical aspects of our problem does not appear to be encouraging. It would seem that there is not much hope for a breakthrough leading to concrete results in the field of church unity. Fortunately, however, this is not the whole story. The relationships between Christians of different confessions have not remained the same but have changed more than anyone could reasonably have expected at the beginning of the ecumenical era. The most impressive illustration of this far-reaching change is the cooperation which has developed in the study and use of the Bible. In 1925, the year in which Stockholm hosted the first world conference of the churches, the German New-Testament scholar Adolf Jülicher described as a illusion the idea that the Bible could act as a uniting link between the churches. "How can the Bible be a link when it is on the basis of divergent interpretations of its text that Christians refuse to recognize one another as Christians?"[6] He stressed especially that there was a profound difference between the Roman Catholic attitude to the Bible, combining liturgical reverence with an insistence that interpretation and distribution must be kept under strict control, and the Protestant desire to put it into the hands of all men and women, so that they might be directly confronted with the word of God. Prof. Jülicher concluded by admitting that some Christian groups might be drawn together by mutual study of the Bible, although he saw no present sign of such a development.

In 1967, two thousand people attended a meeting at the Sorbonne presided over by Cardinal Martin, Metropolitan Meletios and Pastor Boegner, the leaders of the Roman Catholic, Orthodox and Protestant churches in France. They had come together to celebrate the publication of the first book of the ecumenical translation of the Bible. The New Testament was completed by 1972 and the Old Testament by 1975. This ecumenical translation is unique in several ways. Each book was translated by theologians of the different churches working together and, what is even more important, the translation is accompanied by copious notes which are not merely technical in nature, but also provide a substantial exegesis of the text. In only a few places is attention called to varying interpretation given to certain texts by different churches. As the translators state in the preface to the New Testament, they made the great discovery that it was possible to present a common translation, with technical and exegetical notes, without the division and interconfessional disagreement which some people had predicted and many feared.

What had happened was that a new situation had been created by two deep currents in the life of the churches. The first of these was the movement towards "biblical renewal", described by Suzanne de Diétrich in her book of that title. In 1934 already, I was able to observe, in an editorial in *Student World*, that the Bible was becoming a meeting place for members of different churches. This turning towards the Bible was a strong stimulus for the young ecumenical movement.

In the Roman Catholic Church, biblical renewal was first approached very prudently. At the Second Vatican Council, however, to the great surprise even of the Roman Catholic bishops and theologians, that renewal was seen to have been general and substantial to an unexpected degree. The council therefore allotted a place to the Bible in their deliberations such as it had not been given at the council of Trent or at the First Vatican Council. In 1967, Karl Barth, who had been a severe critic of the Roman Catholic attitude to the Bible, said that the Constitution on Divine Revelation was a forward-looking document, and that its main trend was towards the priority (*Vorherrschaft*) of holy scripture, though not towards its supremacy (*Alleinherrschaft*).[7]

The second deep current that had contributed so largely to the great change was, of course, the ecumenical movement itself. Its main objective was not just to persuade the churches to cooperate in the face of the dangers, and the opportunities, of the new era. Its principal motivation was to make manifest that the church of Christ is essentially a single, united body. At the Second Vatican Council, it became clear that the Roman Catholic Church had decided to participate actively in the movement which had developed among the other churches. The combination of these currents, biblical renewal and ecumenism, could not fail to have far-reaching results.

We must recall that the chief concern of the Reformation churches was always to bring the Bible to the people and the people to the Bible, while that of the Roman Catholic Church had always been to maintain the unity of the church in space and time. When in our day we find that the non-Roman churches have become active in striving for church unity, and the Roman Catholic Church has begun to give a central place in its teaching and pastoral work to the holy scriptures, we must conclude that the coming together, the interaction and the cross-fertilization resulting from these two developments, is the most important fact in 20th-century church history.

This does not mean only that the context of the *magisterium* has changed. It means that the role of the *magisterium* is no longer the same. In the Roman Catholic Church, the momentum and inner logic of the "trend towards the Bible" have led to a situation in which practice goes much further than theory. Already in 1967, Oscar Cullmann remarked that the Second Vatican Council had in fact been more under the influence of the Bible than the official Roman Catholic position on this subject seemed to suggest.[8] The de jure position of the Roman church was still that "the task of authentically interpreting the word of God, whether written or handed on, has been entrusted exclusively to the living teaching office of the church".[9] The de facto situation was, however, that French-speaking Christians, possibly to be followed soon by others, were now in possession of a translation of holy scriptures accompanied by all necessary exegesis or interpretation, and that given jointly by theologians of different churches. In a few places, it is true, the reader is given alternative versions, but a number of texts which had earlier given rise to controversy now bear an interpretation accepted by all the collaborating churches. The impression which this gives is that today Christians of different confessions have a common understanding of the scriptures. In the preface to this *Traduction œcuménique de la Bible*, it is noted that responsibility for the translation and interpretation is assumed by those who were involved in the preparation of the work. These included several cardinals and bishops, Protestant church leaders and most of the leading biblical scholars of both confessions. As no church authority has raised any objection to the interpretation it gives, the ecumenical translation can be regarded as at least semi-official, not far removed indeed from being official.

Most of the readers who make grateful use of this edition of the Bible will no doubt come to consider it as their main teaching authority, for this is the channel through which the word of God reaches them. And even if it is not a final interpretation with no possible error in it, it is the most trustworthy to have reached them. It may be a weakness that it has not been given full ecclesiastical sanction, but its strength is that it brings with it the insights of the whole people of God, and thus there emerges what may be called a de facto *magisterium*.

It should be understood that de facto does not mean "illegal". In fact, the churches themselves provide a considerable part of the *magisterium* in de facto form. I am thinking in particular of the many reports on bilateral conversations between the Roman Catholic Church and other churches, which contain the results of the study and dialogue of theologians officially appointed by churches or church federations. None of these reports has yet been adopted by the churches concerned, but they are not without some authority. Cardinal Willebrands considers that they have considerable influence upon theological thinking, and upon the life of the churches.[10]

The same may be said of the study document on "Common Witness". This was prepared at the request of the Working Group of the Roman Catholic Church and the World Council of Churches and was published under the joint auspices of the Roman Catholic Secretariat for Promoting Christian Unity and the World Council's Commission for World Mission and Evangelism. In this connection, the part played by Faith and Order is of great importance. At the meeting of that movement in Lima in 1982, its report on "Baptism, Eucharist and Ministry" was completed. This report resulted from a long process of discussion among theologians of all the main families of Christians. The document is now being submitted to the churches for their approval, and may open up a new chapter in ecumenical relations, which gives it considerable weight.

An initiative of a less official kind, but one approved by the competent episcopal authority of the Roman Catholic Church, is the very substantial publication *The Common Faith*, edited by Johannes Feiner and Lukas Vischer. In this publication, thirty-five Roman Catholic and Protestant theologians have so interpreted the Christian faith as to bring out clearly the convictions held in common while honestly stating points of divergence. These scholars have come to the conclusion that "the affirmations which can be made by all together are more important in quantity and in quality than the still remaining disagreements".

Mention should also be made of the pioneering work of the Groupe des Dombes in France, and of the memorandum on the ministry elaborated by three Roman Catholic and three Protestant ecumenical institutes in German universities. The work of these groups is of major importance in the search for unity.

We do not know yet whether these forward-looking thoughts and affirmations may be considered as the first fruits of what will, at some future date, be a fully recognized teaching – a *magisterium* accepted by all churches. We must hope at least that official church authorities will take concrete steps towards church unity in the very near future. If this is not done, the present uncertainty about the relation between the de jure teaching authority and the de facto authority in the ecumenical area will increase, and there is a possibility that many will transfer their loyalty from the first to the second. In a period such as this, the task of theologians is particularly difficult. They are asked to participate in the formulation of reports or statements which will express the maximum possible agreement that can be reached between their churches and other churches. This task can be performed successfully only if they do not simply reiterate their own traditional positions, but seek common ground and express themselves in common language. Yves Congar has remarked that such agreement cannot simply restate the official doctrinal conceptions of the churches concerned, for if such statements coincided entirely, unity of faith and the union of the churches would already have been accomplished.[11] And until this is so, the statements of theologians are steps on the way to full agreement, which will incorporate the insights of the different churches. Theologians may, indeed must, take the risk of exploring possible new formulations which would be a synthesis of traditional ones. In this light we can understand why the "Observations" that the Sacred Congregation for the Doctrine of the Faith made on the report of the Anglican-Roman Catholic International Commission – where the "Observations" criticized the report for not being in complete agreement with Roman Catholic doctrinal statements – caused so much surprise and dismay.

The ecumenical movement needs theologians who will act as pathfinders. We must not forget that the movement would never have come into existence if such pathfinders had not come forward to explore with courage and imagination and to undertake together a common ecumenical journey. Some of these pioneers were at first considered dangerous, unorthodox and not entirely trustworthy. Years later, they were among the most influential experts at the Second Vatican Council. Pathfinders are indispensable, for there can be no advance towards unity without exploration of new ways of confessing the faith together.

Pathfinders must, however, realize that they are not working for themselves, but for the common cause. They must not become so interested in the technique of producing doctrinal agreements that they forget to ask whether these agreements can be understood and sincerely adopted by the churches concerned. A number of attempts to unite churches have failed because the negotiators treated the problem of disunity as a puzzle to be solved by clever intellectual distinctions and redefinitions which had little meaning for ordinary church members.

The men and women in all churches who have responded to the ecumenical awakening of our time no longer think of their own church as a self-sufficient community competing with other equally self-centred bodies. Nor is there any thought that the weakening of one church is to the advantage of other churches. On the contrary, we have begun to learn again the Pauline lesson of the mysterious coherence of all parts of the body, so that the suffering or rejoicing of one church must have its repercussion on all churches. Even though members of the family have been estranged one from another, the family has not ceased to exist. As we try today to restore the unity of the family, we accept responsibility for one another. The first assembly of the World Council of Churches acknowledged that, owing to our disunity, we had not been receiving the necessary correction from one another. Now, however, that we are again turning towards one another, the process of mutual correction has recommenced. It must not be made inoperative by excessive politeness, for we are not concerned here with diplomacy or politics, but with the true faith and obedience to our Lord. Theologians should therefore have great freedom in expressing their convictions about the teaching of other churches, as well as about that of their own. Theology has a critical function, and there should be no resentment if that function is exercised with the objective of building up the church, and not of destroying it. Further, if some theologians believe that, for the sake of promoting unity, it is their duty to go beyond what is permitted by the official theology and discipline of their church, they should not therefore be excluded from the ecumenical discussion, but should be allowed to make their contribution to it.

NOTES

[1] Franz Leenhardt, *L'Eglise*, Geneva, Labor et Fides, 1978, p.214.
[2] Yves Congar, *Revue des sciences philosophiques et théologiques*, 1976, p.635.
[3] Johannes Willebrands, *Reflections on Twenty Years of the Secretariat for Promoting Christian Unity*, Worcester, MA, Assumption College, 1980.
[4] Congar, *Voices of Unity*, p.29.
[5] Peder Højen and Jürgen Moltmann, *Der Fall Küng*, pp.457,445.
[6] Adolf Jülicher, *Die Eiche*, Munich, Kaiser, 1925, p.276.
[7] Barth, *Ad Limina Apostolorum*, p.58.
[8] Oscar Cullmann, *Die Autorität der Freiheit*, I:196.
[9] *Constitution on Divine Revelation*, 10.
[10] Willebrands, *Reflections on Twenty Years of the Secretariat for Promoting Christian Unity*, 1980.
[11] Congar, *Diversités et Communion*, p.209.

15. *Magistri* as the Fourth Office?

It seems from what we have considered that there is justification for the recognition of the *magistri* as a specific office, in addition to the offices of bishop, priest and deacon, or of pastor, elder and deacon. In view of the importance of the function of the teachers and of the desirability of clarifying their relationship to other offices in the church, the matter seems unavoidable. It is therefore strange that it has been so little discussed in the course of history.

There are of course some examples of such discussion. Origen often spoke of teachers as a distinct office, not to be identified with that of bishops or priests. Harnack collected a number of quotations in which Origen expresses this idea, according to which teachers have a specific task to perform which should be recognized.[1]

In the middle ages, when the universities became the centres of culture with theology as their main concern, the position of theologians became so important that they began to represent an "autonomous *magisterium* in the church, whose authority was not simply a result of the commission received from the hierarchy".[2] According to St Thomas Aquinas, teachers of theology have a *magisterium cathedrae magistralis*, to be distinguished from the *magisterium cathedrae pastoralis* of the hierarchy. *Cathedra* means authority, and the content of authority is *officium doctrinae*. At this time, theologians had even the power to punish. "The University of Paris delivered between 1240 and 1452 about thirty judgments on doctrinal questions with punishments varying from prohibition to teach to excommunication."[3] This extraordinary authority was still defended in the 16th century by the famous theologian Melchior Cano, who said that to contradict the consensus of the theological doctors was very nearly heresy, and that the Lord's words "Who hears you, hears me" refer to theological doctors as well as to the hierarchy. We have noted above that in the 17th century Bossuet based the case for Gallicanism on the statements of the doctors of the Sorbonne. Does this mean that a fourth form of ministry was then, in this way, added to the three traditional ministries? The answer, I believe, is that in practice and de facto this was so, but that in principle and de jure, it was not so, because the

theologians, as theologians, did not become part of the hierarchy. Theo-
retically, they received their authority from the bishops. The formula by
which the chancellor of the university gave the degree of licentiate began
with the words: *Ego, auctoritate apostolica...*[4] Thus the factual autonomy
of the theologians in the middle ages and the functioning of that autonomy as a fourth office had no juridical foundation, so that it could not be
exercised when the hierarchy insisted on its prerogatives.

At the Reformation, Martin Bucer, the Strasbourg Reformer, gave a
very specific answer to the question of the place of theologians in the
church. In his commentary of 1536 on the epistle to the Romans he said
there were four "ministries" in the church; doctors, pastors, governors
and deacons.[5] It is almost certain that Bucer's conception became the
basis of Calvin's theology of church order, for Calvin did not speak of
four ministries before his sojourn in Strasbourg. In 1541, however, when
he returned to Geneva and drafted the "Ordonnances écclésiastiques" he
stated: "First of all there are four orders or offices which our Lord has
instituted for the government of his church, namely the pastors, then the
doctors, next the elders (also called delegates, appointed by the government) and fourthly, the deacons." The task of the doctors is described as
the maintenance of schools in which the holy scriptures are interpreted
and future ministers and catechists are trained. In the editions of the
Institutes which appeared in the following years, we find reference to the
same four ministries,[6] though in one passage only three offices are mentioned.[7]

The Second Helvetic Confession of 1566, which became the common confession of the Swiss Reformed Churches and which was
approved by Reformed churches in France, Hungary, Poland and Scotland,[8] also describes the ministry of the church as being entrusted to
"*episcopi*, presbyters, pastors and doctors". The church order adopted in
Dordrecht in 1619 states in its second article that there are four offices,
pastors, doctors, elders and deacons. There is, however, no evidence that
this theory of a specific office of the doctors was ever translated into
practical and concrete form and, in the long run, most Reformed
churches reverted to the threefold ministry.

In the days of the church conflict in Germany, the concept of a specific order of theologians was reaffirmed. The "Düsseldorfer Thesen" of
1933, signed by prominent Reformed theologians, including Karl Barth,
Wilhelm Niesel and Alfred de Quervain, state that the ministry of the
church is performed by preachers, teachers, elders and deacons. The task
of the teachers is described as the instruction of youth, the training of
ministers and the constant testing of the purity of the church's proclamation in the light of holy scripture.[9] During discussions in the Nether-

lands in the 1930s on a revision of the church order, it was also proposed to recognize the ministry of the doctors as a fourth office. The argument for this was that doctors were specially qualified to deal with the many questions confronting the church, and should be consulted before the representative synods took their decisions on these questions.[10]

On the Roman Catholic side, a very remarkable contribution was made to this discussion by John Cardinal Newman at the end of his life, and after the First Vatican Council. He believed wholeheartedly in the *sensus fidelium* "as a determining factor of the church's fidelity to revelation". He considered that, within the body of the faithful, the *Schola theologorum* was of great importance, as it had "a great role in correcting errors and overly narrow conceptions of the instructions which come to the faithful via active infallibility (i.e. the *magisterium*)".[11] The cardinal thus allotted to theologians a clear and proper role not very different from a specific ministry or office.

More recently, the auxiliary bishop of Paris, Monsignor Daniel Pézeril, wrote that it was urgently necessary for theologians to become more fully aware of their identity in the contemporary church. They were, he said, a body of mediators (*corps intermédiaire*). It is clear that he was proposing the formation of a body which would give theologians a more definite place in the church and a clearer sense of their responsibilities, although he did not state what kind of organization he had in mind.[12]

We must here ask ourselves again whether the terminology used in official statements of the Roman Catholic Church, where bishops are referred to as "authentic teachers",[13] really conveys an adequate conception of the teaching office of the church. Often such statements, in which no mention is made of the role of the theologian, create the impression that that role is of minor importance. It is not made sufficiently clear that there is a considerable difference between the role of the bishop and that of the theological teacher, and that each has his own specific responsibility. A theologian is a full-time teacher who has had a thorough education in his field, and whose energies are concentrated on study and on passing on his theological knowledge to others. The tasks of a bishop are more varied than that. He is of course concerned about the teaching of the church, and has many opportunities to expound it. Teaching is, however, not the sole raison d'être of his office. A bishop may be a good theologian, though this is by no means always the case; but however gifted he is in this direction, his other duties will prevent him from giving the necessary time to theological studies. Pézeril has remarked that it is extremely difficult, if not impossible, for a bishop personally to study the total theological production of our time.[14]

It is therefore difficult to understand why the magisterial role of bishops is affirmed in such a way as to create the impression that theologians are second-class teachers. I am aware that the word "authentic" has various meanings. According to the dictionary, it can mean "having full authority", and it is obviously so used when *Lumen Gentium* speaks of bishops as "authentic teachers, that is, teachers endowed with the authority of Christ". It is strange, however, that nothing is said in this connection about the authority of theologians who give their full time to teaching. An even greater difficulty arises because of another meaning of the word "authentic", namely, "reliable, trustworthy, real and genuine", as opposed to "spurious or counterfeit". The term should therefore be avoided in distinguishing the *cathedra pastoralis* from the *cathedra magistralis*.

The solution does not entail establishing academic doctors and teachers as the ultimate arbiters of truth, thus making of the church a school in which the professors dominate. It should be possible to find words to express the truth that bishops and theologians are each granted their own charism, each receiving a specific gift of grace, and each concerned with the witness of the church, having a place within the one body.

We must, I believe, listen to those voices which have spoken for a definite recognition of the place and role of theologians in the church. In some countries, associations of theologians have already been formed. Such bodies should be created everywhere, and it should be made clear that their purpose is to enable theologians to fulfill their calling within the church and towards the world. If these associations were officially recognized by the church authorities, and if regular contact were established between chosen representatives of the theologians and of church leaders, this would do much to overcome the malaise and tension which are too often seen in the attitude of these two groups to one another, and the church would benefit fully from the specific office entrusted to the theologians.

NOTES

1 Harnack, *Mission und Ausbreitung*, p.343.
2 Roger Gryson, *Journal of Ecumenical Studies*, spring 1982, p.176.
3 P. Schoonenberg, *Journal of Ecumenical Studies*, spring 1982, p.98.
4 Posthumus Meyjes, *Jean Gerson*, p.270.
5 Jaques Courvoisier, *La notion d'Eglise chez Bucer*, Paris, Félix Alcan, 1933, p.88.
6 John Calvin, *Institutes*, 4.3.4.
7 *Ibid.*, 4.4.1.
8 Jaques Courvoisier, *La Confession helvétique postérieure*, Neuchâtel, Delachaux et Niestlé, 1944, p.11.
9 Wilhelm Niesel, *Bekenntnisschriften und Ordnungen*, Zollikon, Evangelischer Verlag, 1938, p.327.
10 A.M. Brouwer, *De Kerkorganisatie der Eerste Eeuw en Wij*, Baarn, Bosch & Keuning, 1937, p.13.
11 Giuseppe Alberigo, *Journal of Ecumenical Studies*, spring 1982, p.128.
12 Daniel Pézeril, *Les théologiens et l'Eglise*, Paris, Beauchesne, 1980, p.62.
13 Second Vatican Council, *Lumen Gentium*, 25; Decree on Bishops, 2, etc.
14 Pézeril, *Les théologiens et l'Eglise*, p.60.

16. Conclusion

Writing about the relations between church leaders and theologians, the Dutch theologian Oepke Noordmans has pointed out that doctors and teachers have always met with difficulties in the church, where their function has never been fully accepted. This may sound like an exaggeration, but we have seen in our short historical survey that there is some truth in it. The place of theologians in the life of the church has never been clearly defined. At times they have been treated as school-teachers, with no other task than that of preparing priests and pastors for their work. At other times they are required to perform the difficult task of formulating the faith. There have been occasions when they have underestimated their mission, and have remained silent when they should have spoken, while on others they act as if they were the only authorized spokesmen of the church. On the whole, the tendency in the Roman Catholic Church has been to limit them to a secondary role, while the Reformation churches have tended to allow them to dominate any discussion on matters of doctrine. As we have seen, however, there are important exceptions.

The conviction underlying this essay is that theologians have their own specific task to perform. They have, as St Paul wrote, their own charism and therefore their own mandate. It is clearly not enough to describe their calling in terms of delegation, so that they appear to be merely auxiliaries of the hierarchy. In 1954, Pius XII said: "Those who are called to teach exercise in the church the office of masters, not in their own name and not because of their scientific competence, but on the basis of the mission they have received from the legitimate *magisterium*."[1] Today, however, this view is no longer generally accepted in the Roman Catholic Church. Joseph Hoffmann has called this conception the "total domestication of theology", and sees as one of the major reasons for tension in the church the fact that the *magisterium*, or at least the Roman curia, pursues an older pattern, while the majority of theologians think in a context in which the problem appears different.[2]

Congar too believes that the time has come to reconsider the relations between theologians and the *magisterium*, and to recognize that the theologians have a charism of their own and a task to perform which should be recognized. This cannot be simply to produce commentaries on papal teachings. The work of the theologians should not be defined only in terms of its relationship to the *magisterium*, even if the *magisterium* is the guardian of the truth. We must not think only of the relationship between these two elements, but must add to them a third conception, that of the apostolic faith. The *magisterium* and theologians must both serve the faith, each in their own way.[3]

That this revaluation of the task of the theologians has begun is a very important development. It should mark the end of an epoch in which the "queen of sciences" was expected to accept orders from the hierarchy, and to devote its attention only to themes indicated by that hierarchy. An epoch, moreover, in which theologians, even if they were of the calibre of St Thomas Aquinas, were not considered to be participants in their own right in the magisterial task.

Theology has a task of its own. It must not only repeat and explain what has been formulated in the past, but also question critically whether the church's teaching and preaching are faithful to the revelation contained in the holy scriptures. It must relate the Christian gospel to new cultural situations and show that it meets new challenges. As Georg Picht has said, our times demand that the prophetic dimension of the Christian witness be heard in the church.[4]

Church leaders and theologians must therefore be considered as partners, and their relationship must be one of collaboration. The church must not become the scene of a monologue by the hierarchy, nor of one by the theologians. The church is essentially dialogical.

To act as serious and responsible partners in that dialogue, theologians must have freedom. But what is the nature of this freedom, and how far should it go? In April 1969 a declaration on "The Freedom of Theologians and of Theology" was issued. It was signed by 1360 Roman Catholic theologians from fifty-three countries, including the present head of the Sacred Congregation for the Doctrine of the Faith; it stated that freedom is a fruit of the liberating message of Jesus himself. The theologians declared that they wished to fulfill their duty of seeking and expressing truth without being hindered by administrative measures and sanctions. They affirmed the teaching authority of the pope and the bishops, but expressed the belief that this pastoral office of witness should not replace, or interfere with, the scientific task of teaching – the task of the theologians.

This seems to me to be the proper basis for an understanding between theologians and church leaders. On the one hand, it requires church leaders to recognize that the specific task of theology can be carried out adequately only in an atmosphere of freedom. The theologians, for their part, have to recognize that church leaders have the pastoral responsibility for the clarity and coherence of the witness of the church to its members, and the world.

This understanding of the connection between freedom and responsibility for the life of the church has also been expressed by theologians of other churches. Karl Barth underlined that theology is a function of the church, existing to render the specific service of continually raising the question of a correct relationship between the church's proclamation and its origin, its objective and its content, which is the word of God. Theology must, however, be conscious of the tradition which lies behind the witness of the church today, and have confidence in it. Theology should not try to impose its findings, but should offer these as advice. It must, however, refuse to be silenced in its critical function by ecclesiastical authorities or anxious church members.[5]

Further, when the *missio canonica* of Hans Küng was withdrawn, the professors of the Roman Catholic and Protestant faculties of theology at the university of Strasbourg declared that a critical reflection on the faith was indispensable, that this reflection must be allowed to develop in full freedom, that there can be no intellectual freedom without responsibility, that theologians must be ready to give an account of their findings before the whole church, and that there are in the church authorized supporters of the church order whose task it is to ensure that the church's witness is true to the faith.[6]

In other words, to demand freedom for theologians is not to open the door to spiritual anarchy. They have no right to freedom unless they are deeply conscious of the serious risks in their activity. The searchlight often falls today on church authorities who seek to maintain their domination over theologians, but theologians too are frequently tempted to monopolize spiritual leadership. Hendrik Kraemer, the Orientalist and missionary, was a layman, but spent a considerable part of his life among theologians. He expressed himself strongly in warning against this danger, speaking of a demonic and tyrannical tendency among theologians to usurp a place which is not theirs. He did not underestimate theology but believed that it must always remain conscious that it is not an end in itself and that its task is to serve and not to dominate.[7]

The accepted way of correcting theological views which contradict central Christian affirmations is a process of mutual criticism within the theological profession. We have shown how certain erroneous tendencies in the theology of the Reformation churches were in fact corrected by the theologians themselves, and have quoted the example of the Dutch bishops who made this point in their letter to Cardinal Ottoviani.

In Roman Catholic literature, however, we often find the formula that the function of theology is to propose to the *magisterium* new interpretations and then to await the approval of the church leaders.[8] I do not think that this does full justice to the theologians' task. New theological ideas have the character of proposals only insofar as they cannot and must not claim to be the last word. Theology must do more than propose ideas, it must attempt to confess the faith.

Theologians must indeed submit their convictions to the judgment of the church and its leadership, and in that sense they must wait for approval. But they have the right and duty to advocate their convictions, and to prepare the way for their acceptance by the church, for what the serious theologian offers is his insight on the revealed truth. That truth demands to be proclaimed, and therefore he cannot remain silent. Clearly, Origen and St Thomas Aquinas, Luther and Karl Barth, Rahner and Schillebeeckx did more than produce proposals. As teachers, they reinterpreted the traditional *didachē* to suit a particular historical and cultural situation. They were seekers who opened up to us realms of revealed truth so far unexplored. Their work has a prophetic dimension in that they point out new tasks for the church.

A good illustration of the creative role of theologians is provided by the development of ecumenism in the Roman Catholic Church, which shows that the *magisterium* may sometimes play a positive and sometimes a negative role.

There were three stages to this development. In the 1920s, a period of many ecumenical initiatives, there were conversations between Roman Catholics and Anglicans at Malines, and a new approach of the Roman church to Anglicanism and Orthodoxy was shown in the activities of the monastery of Amay. Prominent among the pioneers of that time were Fernand Portal and Lambert Beauduin. In 1928, however, the encyclical *Mortalium Animos* and various disciplinary measures taken by the Vatican forced early Roman Catholic ecumenists to give up their plans. Then, in the 1930s a different approach was tried. Paul Couturier organized a Week of Prayer for Unity, and won many supporters of his action by explaining his original ideas in brochures and leaflets. The most substantial contribution at this time, however, was made by Yves Congar who, in his book *Chrétiens désunis,* sought to provide a theological foundation which would permit his church to take a positive attitude to the ecumenical movement. In Germany, Robert Grosche, in his periodical *Catholica*, pointed a way towards a constructive ecumenical dialogue. These various initiatives once more roused negative reactions in the hierarchy, and in some cases called forth disciplinary measures from the highest authorities.

Nevertheless, in the third stage, the years after the second world war, there was a considerable increase in the number of Roman Catholic theologians who were giving special attention to ecumenical issues. Many of them wished to attend the first assembly of the World Council of Churches in Amsterdam in 1948, but this was forbidden to them, as it was again in 1954 at the time of the second assembly. In the meantime, Roman Catholic ecumenists had created an international organization which held conferences regularly. Johannes Willebrands, later Cardinal Willebrands, became its secretary. When the organization had proved its usefulness, Willebrands took up contact with Rome in the person of Augustin Bea, later Cardinal Bea, and laid before him the concerns and hopes of the ecumenists. This time, the reaction was more positive. In 1960, Pope John XXIII decided to create a Secretariat for the Promotion of Christian Unity, of which Cardinal Bea became the first president, and Cardinal Willebrands the second. Further, observers from other churches were invited to attend the Second Vatican Council, and cooperative relations were established with the World Council of Churches. Most important of all, in 1964 the Second Vatican Council adopted the Decree on Ecumenism, thus showing that the Roman Catholic Church was ready to accept its share in the ecumenical task.

Thus, by their tenacious and patient advocacy of their urgent task, and in spite of opposition, theologians had paved the way for a decision, and the *magisterium* had confirmed it.

What, then, is the true task of the *magisterium*? In speaking of the teaching authority in and of the church today, we have to be aware that there are, in the minds of many of our contemporaries, two erroneous conceptions of authority. One of them is the idea that authority belongs entirely to the past and that talk of authority in the church simply reveals that the church is an anachronism. Modern intellectuals with bookcases full of the works of Voltaire, Shelley, Kierkegaard, Tolstoi, Marx, Nietzsche and Freud have been heavily inoculated against the truth proclaimed by the church, and there is a deep mistrust of authority in all its forms in the culture of today. The church, however, speaks for the Messiah, of whom it was rightly said that he "spoke with authority and not as the scribes", and of whom his disciples said that his words were words of eternal life. If any church is unable or unwilling to speak with that authority, it has become a society for debating religious questions, or a club where religious feelings are cultivated. It has lost all connection with the church that was born in Jerusalem one Whitsuntide.

The form in which the authority of the gospel and its implications are presented today cannot, however, be the same as in the past. Authority of the type at one time held by kings, by parents, and above all by the church, used to be accepted without question and for ever. The progressive emancipation of the individual has now undermined authority in this form. People today are not willing to surrender their right to ask critical questions on any statement or instruction issued in the name of authority. When the voice of authority says, or seems to say, "This is true because I say it", the response is likely to be, "This truth can become mine only if you convince my reason and my conscience". The word of the *magisterium* is not the last word, but one leading to intensive discussion. Thus *Roma locuta, causa finita* is a conception of the past – and this applies equally to any church in which decisions of the church authorities were in the past obeyed without question. In this situation, the task of the *magisterium* has become much more difficult, for if its solemn statements on issues of faith and life fail to convince the majority of church members, it has undermined its own authority.

It is therefore of great importance that members should feel that the leaders of the church are speaking for them all, and not simply for any given category among churchmen. Members must see that their leaders are speaking for and with the whole church, and not as a teaching church (*ecclesia docens*), sharply divided from and standing over against a learning church (*ecclesia discens*).

The role to be played by church leaders has been clearly indicated in the New Testament. In the earliest of the New Testament writings, the first epistle to the Thessalonians, there is a clear reference to them. No specific office had yet been established, but there were men who were working hard among the faithful, leading them and admonishing them when necessary.[9] Church leaders were not merely administrators, but were also concerned about the faith and life of the people. They were not alone in this, of course, for St Paul said more than once that all members of the church family were to exhort and admonish one another,[10] and underlined that the admonishing or warning was to be done in a fraternal and not in an inimical spirit.

Almost all the New Testament authors used the image of the shepherd with his flock, speaking of the loving care of the Good Shepherd for every one of his sheep, and his particular concern that the flock should stay together. Church leaders were expected to gather together the church members, who were always in danger of being dispersed. They were responsible for the coherence and unity of the church. We read of the threat of false teachings breaking into the church from outside, but also of the menace of heresy within it.[11] It is, however, emphasized that leadership in the church must not mean domination. The same Peter to whom the Lord said, "Feed my sheep", warned the elders of the church not to tyrannize those allotted to their care.[12]

One cannot choose to be a church leader – such leadership is a charism, a gift from the Holy Spirit. When, in the twelfth chapter of the first epistle to the Corinthians, St Paul enumerates *charismata*, he includes *kybernesis*, the quality of being a helmsman.[13] The leaders in the church have the duty of steering it in the right direction.

Another important task of these leaders is expressed by the term *oikonomia*, which is unfortunately often translated in such a way that its original meaning is obscured. *Oikonomia* is household management, and the *oikonomos* is the steward. In 1 Corinthians 9:17 St Paul's vocation is described as stewardship, and in the epistle to Titus the *episkopos* or bishop is called "God's steward". He is not, however, the only steward. In the first epistle of Peter, all members of the church are urged to participate in the God-given *oikonomia* in its various forms, and in every possible way.

What, then, do we learn from the insights of these New Testament writers about the relationship which should exist between the *magisterium* and the *magistri*? The answer, I think, can be summarized in the following points:

1. Contained in the mandate of church leaders is the duty of reminding theologians that, while pluralism in theology is inevitable and desirable at this time, it has its limits. All theologies must proclaim the central beliefs of the faith so that the total witness of the church may be true to its origin, and so that the world is not left in uncertainty as to what the church stands for.

2. It is also within the mandate of church leaders to ensure that the existence of different theological schools or tendencies does not lead to the formation of partisan groups, each seeking to dominate the church. Church leaders should not endeavour to impose uniformity, but they have the right and duty to warn theologians against any theological exclusiveness which threatens to disrupt the unity of the church.

3. Church leaders, standing as they do at the helm, must give a sense of direction to theologians by making them constantly aware of the great problems which face, or will shortly face, the church, as it confronts the increasingly secularized and paganized world, with its spiritual and moral disintegration.

4. It is the great task of church leaders to ensure that the members of the community share with one another the gifts of God. They have to help each theologian to find his rightful place in the church, so that there shall be neither theological unemployment, where these thinkers are performing no useful task, nor theological frozen credits, where the church is deprived of the use of the spiritual and mental capital which their insights represent. Church leaders must encourage theologians to leave

their ivory towers, to cooperate with one another, and above all to cooperate with the laity in clarifying the church's message to the world and its task there.

All the duties that I have mentioned are of a pastoral nature, and are to be carried out by guiding, exhorting and encouraging the church members. But has the *magisterium* not a further task, one of a more juridical nature – that of taking disciplinary measures against theologians whose teaching contradicts the official teaching of the church? This is indeed a responsibility of the church authorities, but it is a secondary one, which must not dominate the policy of the leadership. In the course of church history, the disciplinary function of the church has been so exaggerated that the *magisterium* has come to be seen as a tribunal of judges rather than as a fraternal body with the task of advising, in keeping with St Paul's words that the disobedient should be treated as members of the family.[14] The disappearance of the Inquisition unfortunately did not bring about the disappearance of its approach, with its juridical and suspicious attitude, and its tendency to condemn any new formulation of the faith. In a penetrating study, Prof. Giuseppe Alberigo has shown that the style in which the papacy was conducted in the 19th and the first half of the 20th century was conditioned by the idea that the time had passed for charity and gentleness, and that harshness and condemnation had become regrettable but nevertheless imperative necessities.[15] In 1832, Pope Gregory XVI quoted St Paul's question, "Shall I come to you with a rod, or with love in the spirit of gentleness?"[16] and made it clear that, to his mind, the situation of the church was such that indulgence must be set aside and the rod must be used.[17] In the above-mentioned study, Prof. Alberigo went on to say that for the following 130 years, the Roman Catholic *magisterium* was dominated by the struggle against error, and that it was therefore a new day when, just before the Second Vatican Council, Pope John XXIII said: "Today the Bride of Christ prefers to apply the medicine of mercy rather than that of severity." The Second Vatican Council sought to express this positive concept of the *magisterium*, and avoided condemnations. After the council, however, there was a return to the old methods of investigation, intervention and disciplinary measures. Prof. Alberigo's conclusion was: "Catholicism must leave behind the dark days when church discipline was maintained by trials and condemnations that induced fear and severity. This is vital if the church is still to have a theology in the future." His words are as true for the other churches as they are for the church of Rome.

There are of course extreme situations in which the integrity or even the very existence of the church as witness to the gospel is at stake. When such a *status confessionis* arises, it is particularly important that the teaching authority of the church should react in such a way that it is heard as the voice of the whole church, and not as that of a small group of leaders speaking for themselves. Both theologians and laymen should therefore be associated with the official leaders in confessing the faith in critical circumstances.

With regard to the teaching of any theologian which raises questions in the minds of the *magisterium*, Prof. Leonard Swidler has proposed that recommendations should be sent to the Sacred Congregation for the Doctrine of the Faith, urging that, if it is deemed important to focus on the work of a particular theologian, the congregation should not only call in the theologian in question and its own consultants, but should bring together a group, selected on a worldwide basis, of the best theological scholars whose opinions are pertinent to the matter at issue, and who represent a variety of methodologies and approaches. He points out that this procedure is by no means new, as it is precisely that used at the Second Vatican Council.[18] This seems to me to be a wise suggestion which should also be followed by other churches.

Looking back, then, on the somewhat tumultuous history of relations between theologians and the *magisterium*, we can see clearly that they need one another. They need one another because both are in danger of forgetting the limits of their tasks, and therefore both need a constructively critical partner. "They must stimulate each other and critically, attentively, point each other to the *sensus fidelium* – the faith of the whole church."[19] Theology and the *magisterium* need one another also because only through their close cooperation can the most serious problems of the church's life and witness be solved. Great moments in the history of the church have been those when the *magisterium* called upon theologians to make their contribution, or when they came spontaneously to the rescue of the church.

There are three examples which might be given – three events of exceptional significance in the history of the church in the 20th century. In 1934, when the Protestant churches in Germany were in danger of being overwhelmed by a wave of syncretism resulting from what was known as the German Christian movement, a group of theologians, which included among others Karl Barth and Hans Asmussen, took the initiative of gathering together those who defended the integrity of the church on the basis of the Barmen Declaration of faith, and thus brought into being the Confessing Church. Another striking example may be found in the widespread and intensive cooperation between church leaders, theologians and laymen which was one of the most significant features of the ecumenical movement in its early days. The pioneer in this new mobilization, coordination and management of all resources was

Dr J.H. Oldham. During the preparations for the Life and Work conference held in Oxford in 1937, he succeeded in persuading theologians, Christian laymen of many professions and church leaders to enter into dialogue with one another.

The outstanding example in the life of the Roman Catholic Church which was of importance in this way was the Second Vatican Council. Before it took place, there had been no real dialogue between Roman Catholic theologians and the authorities of their church. It seemed almost a miracle therefore that the council became the meeting place of the *magistri* and the *magisterium*. Because of the desire for a real *aggiornamento* and the imaginative policy of Pope John XXIII, theologians were here given a remarkable opportunity to fulfill their task and follow their calling.

Those who took part in those creative developments thought that the mutual understanding and harmonious collaboration established between church leaders and theologians would have lasting results. But this was not the case. After a few years, the old problem of relationship appeared in a new form. This was inevitable, as we have seen, because the problem assumes a different form in each historical period. The real issue was whether church leaders and theologians, and indeed the whole church, could recognize in each new situation a *kairos*, a time of crisis and opportunity which again demanded the mobilization of the whole church. Only the spiritually blind can deny that the 1980s are a time of acute crisis in the life of the church, but they are also a time of remarkable new opportunities, and therefore a time to ensure that all spiritual gifts are used to the full and "for the common good".[20]

The earliest reference in the New Testament to church leaders is to be found in the fifth chapter of the first epistle to the Thessalonians, the oldest of the New Testament documents. The leaders were then described in very general terms, and there was no mention of different functions or titles. There was, however, already a strong emphasis on the gratitude and loyalty which should be shown to these leaders by Christians. St Paul wrote: "We beg you, brothers, to acknowledge those who are working so hard among you, and in the Lord's fellowship are your leaders and counsellors. Hold them in the highest possible esteem and affection for the work they do."[21] Now, it is very significant that St Paul stated almost immediately afterwards: "Do not stifle inspiration and do not despise prophetic utterances, but bring them all to the test and then keep what is good in them and avoid the bad of whatever kind."[22] This passage shows that, in St Paul's mind, church members were to treat their leaders with respect and take their exhortations and warnings seriously. At the same time, they had to be aware of the constant activity of the Holy Spirit –

the literal rendering of verse 19 is: "Do not quench the Spirit." For the Spirit is the giver of new life. If there is no expectation that the Spirit will act, and no readiness to receive the new inspiration from him, the church has lost its way. Both of St Paul's exhortations were addressed to the church as a whole, and both must be heard anew by each new generation if the church is to accomplish its God-given mission.

NOTES

[1] Pius XII, in *Les théologiens et l'Eglise*, p.100.
[2] Hoffmann, in *Les théologiens et l'Eglise*, p.101.
[3] Congar, *Revue des sciences philosophiques et théologiques*, 1976, p.112.
[4] Georg Picht, *Was ist Theologie?*, Stuttgart, Kreuz-Verlag, 1977, p.404.
[5] Karl Barth, *Einführung in die Evangelische Theologie*, Zurich, EVZ-Verlag, 1963, 1962, pp.49-52.
[6] *Der Fall Küng*, p.302.
[7] Hendrik Kraemer, *De Kerk in Beweging*, The Hague, Boekencentrum 1947, pp.117,138,183.
[8] Schoof, *Aggiornamento*, p.278.
[9] 1 Thess. 5:12.
[10] Col. 3:16; 1 Thess. 5:14; Rom. 15:14.
[11] Acts 20:28-31.
[12] 1 Peter 5:1-3.
[13] 1 Cor. 12:28.
[14] 2 Thess. 3:15, New English Bible.
[15] Giuseppe Alberigo, *Journal of Ecumenical Studies*, spring 1982.
[16] 1 Cor. 4:21.
[17] Encyclical *Mirari Vos*.
[18] Leonard Swidler, *Journal of Ecumenical Studies*, spring 1982, p.242.
[19] P. Schoonenberg, *Journal of Ecumenical Studies*, spring 1982, p.117.
[20] 1 Cor. 12:7.
[21] 1 Thess. 5:12-13, New English Bible.
[22] 1 Thess. 5:19-22.